Settlebeck High School

Long Lane, Sedbergh, Cumbria LA10 5AL Tel. 05396 20383 Fax 05396 21024
Headteacher Mason Minnitt M.A.

		EXCELLENT	2000/01
			2001/02
			2002/03
			2003/04
			2004/05
			2005/06
			2006/07
		Book Number A2	

Schools Curriculum Award

First published in 2000 by
Stanley Thornes (Publishers) Ltd

Reprinted in 2001 by
Nelson Thornes Ltd
Delta Place
27 Bath Road
CHELTENHAM
GL53 7TH
United Kingdom

01 02 03 04 05 / 10 9 8 7 6 5 4 3 2

A catalogue record for this book is available from the British Library.

ISBN 0 7487 5396 6

Original design concept by Studio Dorel
Cover photographs: Pictor International
Artwork by Oxford Illustrators
Cartoons by Clinton Banbury
Typeset by Tech Set Ltd, Gateshead, Tyne & Wear
Printed and bound in Italy by G. Canale & C.S.p.A., Borgaro T.se, Turin

Acknowledgements

The publishers thank the following for permission to reproduce copyright material:

Ace Photo Agency, back cover; Apple, p. 64; Bubbles Photolibrary p. 176 (left – Mach Mal Pause, right – Jennie Woodcock); David Hoffman, p. 132 (bottom); John Walmsley Photolibrary, p. 156; Leslie Garland Picture Library, pp. 78, 132 (top); Martyn Chillmaid, pp. 25, 80, 81, 86, 88; Science Photolibrary, p. 113 (Professor Peter Goddard); Stone, pp. cover spine (Lori Adamski Peek), 10 (Ken Fisher); Telegraph Colour Library, p. 23 (Oliver Ribardiere); Trip, pp. 134 (H Rogers), 136 (Dinardia), 137 (I Deineko); Walls Birdseye, p. 74.

The publishers have made every effort to contact copyright holders, but apologise if any have been overlooked.

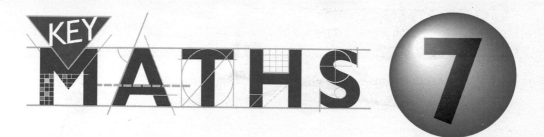

KEY MATHS 7

▶ **David Baker**
The Anthony Gell School, Wirksworth

▶ **Paul Hogan**
St. Wilfrid's Church of England High School, Blackburn

▶ **Barbara Job**
Formerly of Christleton County High School, Chester

T

Contents

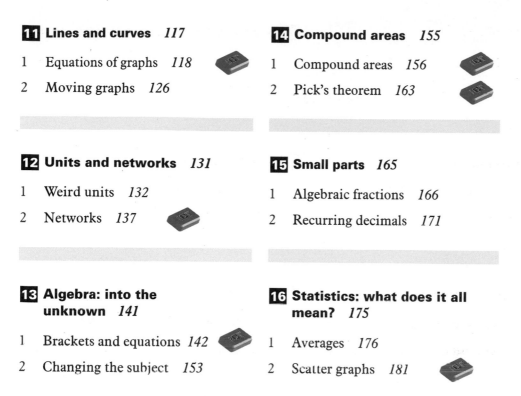

 # Statistics

One is not a prime number

One is sometimes called unity

One is the first square number and the first triangular number

One is the first odd number

Multiplication or division by one has no effect

1 Statistical diagrams

The contestant in a quiz game has one minute to answer ten questions.
The clock shows how much time he has left.
He has just over half a minute left.

Pie-chart	A **pie-chart** shows how something is divided up.

The angle at the centre is 360°
The angle of the sector represents the number of items in the sector.

Example

40 people are asked which news programme they watch.
Draw a pie-chart for this data.

Programme	BBC	ITV	Sky	Other
Number of people	20	10	5	5

20 is a half of 40 so BBC gets $\frac{1}{2}$ of the pie-chart.

Similarly ITV gets $\frac{1}{4}$ of the pie-chart.
Sky and Other each get $\frac{1}{8}$ of the pie-chart.

Type of news programme

Exercise 1:1

1 60 people were asked which TV channel they were watching at 7 pm yesterday. The table shows the results.

Channel	BBC	ITV	Sky
Number of people	15	30	15

Draw a pie-chart to show this information.

2 Lorna earns £120 per week. This is how she spends her money.

	Rent	Clothes	Food	Other
Amount (£)	60	15	30	15

Draw a pie-chart to show this data.

Sometimes the data does not work out into simple fractions.
When this happens you have to work out the angles.

Tara did a survey of 180 pupils. She asked how they got to school.
These are her results.

Transport	bus	car	cycle	walk
Pupils	76	31	18	55

A full turn is **360°**. The 360° must represent **180** pupils.
This means each pupil gets **360° ÷ 180 = 2°**
Work out the angle for each type of transport. Do this in a table.

Transport	Number of pupils	Working	Angle
bus	76	76 × 2° =	152°
car	31	31 × 2° =	62°
cycle	18	18 × 2° =	36°
walk	55	55 × 2° =	110°

Check the angles add up to 360°
152° + 62° + 36° + 110° = 360°   ✓

Draw a circle of about 4 cm radius. Mark the centre. Draw a line to the top of the circle. Measure the first angle, 152°

Carry on until you have drawn all the angles. Label each sector. Give your pie-chart a title.

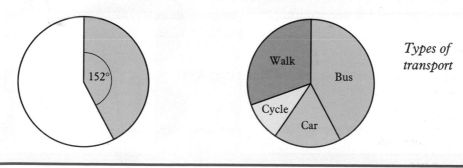

Types of transport

3 360 people were asked which type of heating they used. This table shows the results.

Type of fuel	oil	gas	solid fuel	electricity
People	95	166	58	41

   a Work out the angle for each person.
   b Draw a pie-chart to show the data.

4 The table shows the amount of each type of fuel sold by a garage in one week.

Type of fuel	lead-replacement petrol	unleaded petrol	diesel
Amount (1000s of gallons)	38	87	55

   a Work out the angle for each 1000 gallons.
   b Draw a pie-chart to show the data.

5 The table shows the bill for mending Sara's washing machine.

Labour	Parts	Call out charge
£32	£15	£25

Draw a pie-chart to show this data.

6 The table shows the number of racquets that a sports shop sold in one month.

Type	Number sold
tennis	156
squash	290
badminton	222
raquetball	52

Draw a pie-chart to show this data.

Example   A health centre surveyed
the distance patients travelled
to the surgery.
180 patients were involved in
the survey.
The pie-chart shows the results.

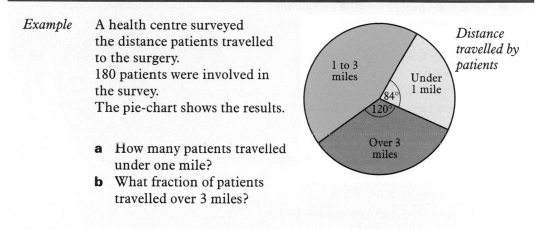

*Distance
travelled by
patients*

a How many patients travelled
under one mile?
b What fraction of patients
travelled over 3 miles?

a In the pie-chart, 360° show all **180** patients
so 1 patient is represented by **360° ÷ 180 = 2°**
The angle of the sector of the pie-chart for under one mile is 84°
The number of patients that travelled under one mile is 84° ÷ 2 = 42

b The sector for over 3 miles has an angle of 120°
The total angle is 360° so the fraction is $\frac{120}{360} = \frac{1}{3}$
The fraction of patients that travelled over 3 miles is $\frac{1}{3}$

7 The pie-chart shows the results
of a survey of 1080 people.
The survey asked about the types of
book that people read.

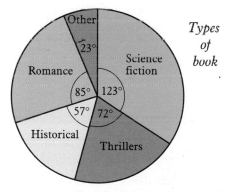

*Types
of
book*

Copy the table.
Use the pie-chart to fill it in.

Type	science fiction	thrillers	historical	romance	other
Number					

8 The pie-chart shows the proportion, by weight, of the contents of a type of cereal.

   a What fraction of the cereal is
   (1) fibre
   (2) protein?

   b Lisa has a serving of 100 g for breakfast. How many grams of fat are there in Lisa's serving?

   c Work out the angle for carbohydrate.

   d George's serving has 117 g of carbohydrate. What angle represents 1 g of carbohydrate for George's serving?

   e What size serving did George have?

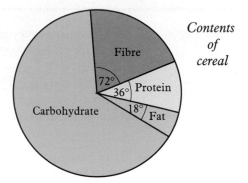

Contents of cereal

9 The pie-chart shows the grades that students achieved in their A-level exams.

   a What fraction of students scored a C grade?

   b What fraction of students scored either an A or a B grade?

   c 14 students scored a grade A. How many students are represented by the pie-chart?

   d How many students scored a D grade?

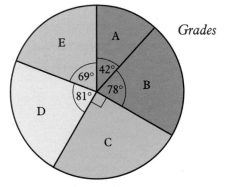

Grades

10 The pie-chart shows how a company spends its income.

   a What fraction of the income is spent on raw materials?

   b The profit is £2 600 000 What is the total income of the company?

   c How much is spent on raw materials?

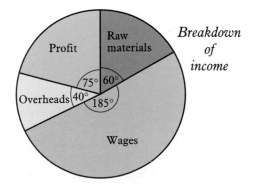

Breakdown of income

Stem and leaf diagram	A **stem and leaf diagram** shows the shape of a set of data. It is like a bar chart with the numbers forming the bars.

Example

These are the times, in minutes, taken by 10 pupils to solve a page of puzzles.

18   25   23   31   20   19   28   35   22   33

Draw a stem and leaf diagram to show these times.

Each number has a tens digit and a unit digit   e.g.   **18, 35**

The tens digits form the stems, the units digits form the leaves.

Stem	Leaf
1	8 9
2	5 3 0 8 2
3	1 5 3

Times taken by pupils to solve puzzles

Now put the leaves (units) in size order.

Give your diagram a title and a key.

Stem	Leaf
1	8 9
2	0 2 3 5 8
3	1 3 5

Key: 2|3 means 23 minutes

Exercise 1:2

1 The stem and leaf diagram shows the ages, in years, of a group of people.

Ages of people

Stem	Leaf
1	4 7 8 8 9
2	0 1 3 5 5 8
3	4 5 8 9
4	0 2 3 5
5	2 7

Key: 4|2 means 42 years

   a What is the age of
   (1) the youngest
   (2) the eldest?
   b How many people are in the group?

2 These are the numbers of beds sold each week by a store during a twelve-week period.

25   15   30   27   21   17   15   36   29   30   17   22

Draw a stem and leaf diagram to show this data.

3 These are the highest daytime temperatures, in °C, in Adeney during a two-week period in August.

18 20 19 21 25 17 23
22 16 17 29 18 24 30

Draw a stem and leaf diagram to show this data.

These are the weekly attendances at a sports club for eight weeks.

351 169 265 291 304 178 250 265

With larger numbers you need to decide how to split them into a stem and leaves.

Use the hundreds unit for the stem.

Stem	Leaf
1	69 78
2	65 91 50 65
3	51 4

Putting the leaves in order gives the final diagram.

Weekly attendance

Stem	Leaf
1	69 78
2	50 65 65 91
3	4 51

Key: 2|65 means 265

---

4 Dawn has done a survey on the miles travelled by people on an intercity train. These are her results.

234 189 306 271 165 284 316 166 217 178 305

Draw a stem and leaf diagram to show this data.

5 Rory measures the lengths in centimetres of 20 earthworms. These are his results.

7.5 4.8 3.9 5.1 3.5 4.7 8.2 4.3 6.0 5.7
8.5 4.6 7.7 3.8 4.2 5.4 4.8 6.1 4.2 5.8

Draw a stem and leaf diagram for this data. Use the units for the stem and the first decimal place for the leaves. Don't forget a key.

Stem	Leaf
3	9 8 …
4	8 … …
…	… … …

Some stem and leaf diagrams have a
small number of stems and a lot of leaves.
This diagram shows the ages of people
in a block of retirement flats.

Stem	Leaf
6	1 2 3 3 5 6 7 8 8 9
7	0 2 2 3 3 4 5 6 7 7 8
8	1 1 4 6 8 9 9

For this type of diagram you split
each stem number into two rows.
The first row contains the
leaves 0, 1, 2, 3 and 4.
The second row contains
the leaves 5, 6, 7, 8 and 9.

Stem	Leaf
6	1 2 3 3
6	5 6 7 8 8 9
7	0 2 2 3 3 4
7	5 6 7 7 8
8	1 1 4
8	6 8 9 9

Key: 7|2 means 72

6 Mr Williams has to write 24 reports for his form.
He recorded the time it took to write each report.
These are his times in minutes.

7.8 6.3 7.2 8.1 6.5 7.0 7.7 6.0 8.4 7.1 6.7 8.9
6.8 7.5 7.2 8.2 8.9 7.1 6.6 7.4 6.5 7.5 7.0 6.8

Draw a stem and leaf diagram to show his results.
Use two rows for each different stem value.

7 Tom is testing a machine to check
that it delivers the correct weight
of sweets.
He takes a sample of 20 packets and
weighs them.
These are his results.
The weights are in grams.

248 244 237 240 237
245 240 247 236 249
235 234 246 250 232
238 245 241 239 251

Using two rows for each stem, draw a stem and leaf diagram to show
Tom's data.
Use the values 23, 24, ... as the stems.

2 Two-way tables

Harry has used this group of people for a survey.
He wants to be able to read how many adults, children, males and females there are.
He needs to use a two-way table.

Two-way table

A **two-way table** can show two types of information at once.
The rows show one piece of information.
The columns show the second piece of information.

This is Harry's table.
Look at the rows of the table.

The row in red gives the number of males.
Number of **males** = 25 + 36 = **61**

	Children	Adults
Male	25	36
Female	31	28

The row in blue gives the number of females.
Number of females = 31 + 28 = 59

This is Harry's table again.
Look at the columns.

The column in green gives the number of children.
Number of children = 25 + 31 = 56

	Children	Adults
Male	25	36
Female	31	28

The column in purple gives the number of adults.
Number of adults = 36 + 28 = 64

The total number of people represented in the table = 25 + 36 + 31 + 28 = 120

Exercise 1:3

1 Stanthorne High is having a special
activities afternoon.
Pupils have to choose two activities each.
They must choose either painting or
cookery for the first session.
They must choose tennis or rounders for the
second session.
The table shows what the pupils choose to do.

	Tennis	Rounders
Painting	15	29
Cookery	21	37

Write down how many pupils:
- **a** chose cookery
- **b** chose tennis
- **c** chose rounders
- **d** there were in total.

2 The table gives the number of pensioners in each of three villages.

	Male	Female
Dartley	125	164
Markton	109	148
Southfield	143	156

Write down how many pensioners:
- **a** are male
- **b** live in Markton
- **c** are female and live in Dartley
- **d** live in either Markton or Southfield
- **e** are male and live in Southfield
- **f** there are altogether.

3 The table gives the ages and wages of the employees of a factory.

Age in years

		up to 30	31–50	over 50
	up to £200	48	21	7
Wage per week	£201–£400	17	59	32
	over £400	4	16	11

Write down how many employees:
- **a** there are altogether
- **b** earn up to £200
- **c** are over 50
- **d** are 50 or less
- **e** earn more than £200
- **f** are 30 or less and earn more than £200.

Example

Diane has done a survey into eye colour. She asked 55 pupils.
25 of them were boys.
19 pupils had blue eyes and 24 had brown eyes.
Fill in the missing numbers in this table.

Eye colour

	blue	brown	other
boys girls	5		9

Look at the boys row. There are 25 boys in the survey. $5 + 9 = 14$
So the missing number is $25 - 14 = $ **11**

Look at the blue eyes column. 19 pupils had blue eyes.
The missing number is $19 - 5 = 14$

Look at the brown eyes column. The top number is **11**. 24 pupils had brown eyes.
The bottom number is $24 - 11 = 13$

Look at the girls row. There are $55 - 25 = 30$ girls. $14 + 13 = 27$
So the missing number is $30 - 27 = $ **3**

The completed table is:

Eye colour

	blue	brown	other
boys	5	11	9
girls	14	13	3

Check to see that the total number of pupils is correct.
$5 + 11 + 9 + 14 + 13 + 3 = 55$ ✓

---

4 Diners at a restaurant choose one starter and one main course from this menu.

One night there were 48 diners. 31 chose pate.
21 chose chicken and 7 chose the vegetarian stir-fry.

Starters
Melon
Pate

Main Courses
Chicken
Salmon
Vegetarian stir-fry

a Copy this table. Fill it in.

Main course

		chicken	salmon	vegetarian
Starters	melon pate	16		3

b Use your table to write down the number of diners who chose:

(1) melon and chicken   (2) pate and salmon.

5 Pupils in Years 7, 8 and 9 took part in a voluntary fast for charity.
320 pupils took part. 192 of these were girls.
There were 36 boys in Year 7 and 55 in Year 9 taking part.
80 Year 7 pupils took part and 109 Year 8 pupils.

a Copy this table. Fill it in.

	Year 7	Year 8	Year 9
boys girls			

b Use your table to write down the number of:

(1) boys in Year 8 taking part   (2) girls in Year 9 taking part.

6 Farmer Joe has 280 animals.
49 are cows, 180 are sheep and the rest are pigs.
Half the sheep together with 18 cows and some pigs are to be sold.
Farmer Joe is selling a total of 131 animals.

a Copy this table. Fill it in.

	cows	sheep	pigs
to keep to sell			

b Use your table to write down the total number of:

(1) pigs   (2) animals to be kept.

7   A club offering swimming or gym facilities has 195 members.
Of the 99 swimming members, 40 are male.
72 men use the gym.

Design a table to show this data. Fill it in.

8   Kirsty has done a survey on the hair of 100 people.
She has filled in this form for each pupil.

Colour of hair: Blonde ☐   Brown ☐   Black ☐

Type of hair: Curly ☐   Wavy ☐   Straight ☐

These are some facts from her survey:

Number with blonde hair = 21   Number with straight blonde hair = 10
Number with wavy hair = 41   Number with curly blonde hair = 3
Number with black wavy hair = 16   Number with black straight hair = 6
Number with straight hair = 34   Number with black curly hair = 10

Design a table to show this data. Fill it in.

9   There are 300 delegates on a management training course.
They all complete a questionnaire.
In the questionnaire one question asks if they come from a private company, a public company or are freelance.
Another question asks if they have travelled to the course by car, coach or train.

Of the 134 people from private companies, 42 travelled by train and 24 travelled by coach.
Out of the total of 98 who travelled by train, 6 were freelance.
Of the 116 people that came by car, 31 were from public companies.
The total number of people from public companies was 129.

Design a table to show this data. Fill it in.

2 Symmetry

1 **Reflection**

2 **Rotation**

Two is the only
even prime number

Computers work in
base 2, called binary

Any number multiplied by
two is the same as the
number added to itself

The most common type
of symmetry divides a
shape into two parts

e, a very important
number in maths, is a bit
more than two. It is
2.718 281 8…

1 Reflection

A kaleidoscope is a child's toy.
It gives a picture with lots of
reflections.
The mirrors in a kaleidoscope are
set at an angle.
The mirror lines aren't just
vertical and horizontal.
You can do reflections in diagonal
mirror lines.

Object

The shape that you start with is called the **object**.

Image

The shape that you get after doing a reflection is called the
image.

For a diagonal line of symmetry the image is still exactly the
same distance from the mirror line as the object.

Example

Draw the image of the object
after reflection in the mirror line.

Look at each square separately.
Make sure that the image is the
same distance from the mirror
line as the object.

You can use a mirror to help you.
What you see in the mirror must
be exactly what you have drawn.

You can also use tracing paper to
help.

Trace the object and the mirror line.

Turn the tracing paper over and put the traced mirror line on
top of the actual mirror line.

Your tracing of the object should cover the image that you
have drawn.

Exercise 2:1

1 For each part:
   (1) copy the object and the mirror line on to squared paper
   (2) draw the image after reflection.

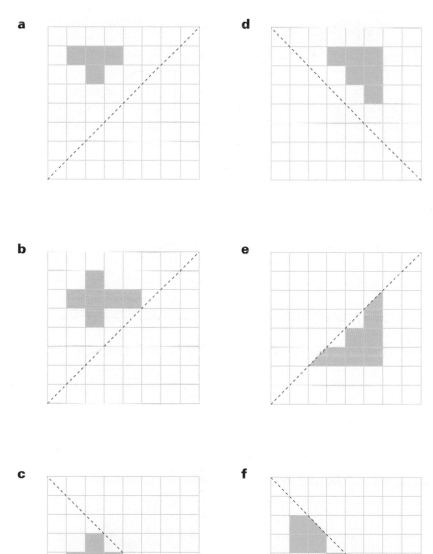

a

b

c

d

e

f

2 For each part:
   (1) copy the object and the mirror line on to squared paper
   (2) draw the image after reflection.

a   **c**

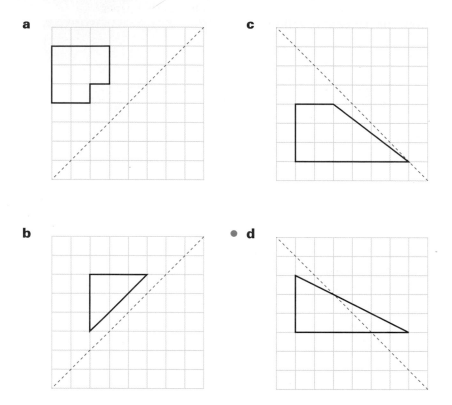

b   **● d**

3 For each part:
   (1) copy the diagram on to squared paper
   (2) fill in two more squares so that the diagram is symmetrical.

a   **b**

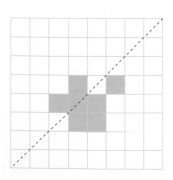
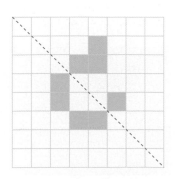

4 For each part:
  (1) copy the diagram on to squared paper
  (2) fill in three more squares so that the diagram is symmetrical.

a **b**

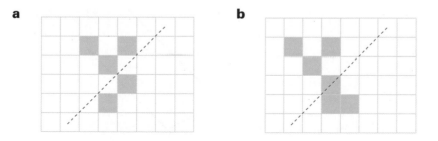

5 These patterns have two lines of symmetry.
  For each part:
  (1) copy the diagram on to squared paper
  (2) complete the diagram so that it is symmetrical.

a **b**

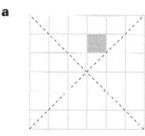
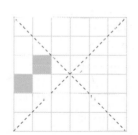

6 These patterns have four lines of symmetry.
  For each part:
  (1) copy the diagram on to squared paper
  (2) complete the diagram so that it is symmetrical.

a **b**

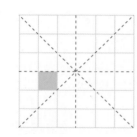
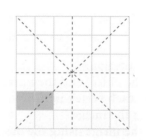

You can label the vertices of a shape with capital letters.

This is shape ABCD

When you reflect a shape labelled like this you need a way of labelling the image.

The image of A is labelled A′.
The image of B is B′.
The image of C is C′.
The image of D is D′.

When you do reflections of shapes like this, reflect each vertex separately and then join up the image at the end.

Count diagonal squares to check that the image of each vertex is the same distance from the mirror as the object vertex.

This method has the advantage that you can easily see where each vertex has moved because the labels keep the original letters of the vertices.

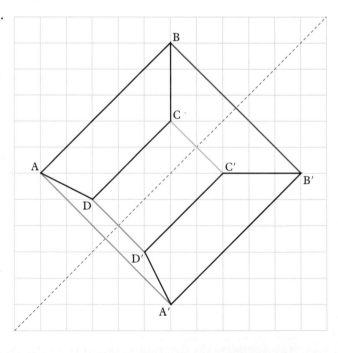

Exercise 2:2

For each question:
a copy the object and the mirror line on to squared paper
b reflect each vertex in turn
c join up the image
d label the image using the dash notation.

1

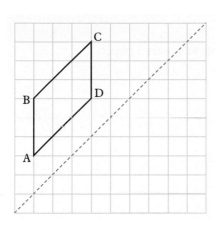

4

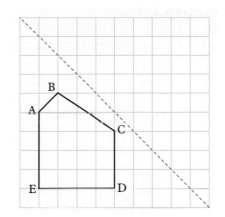

2

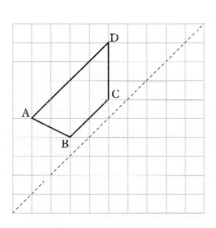

5

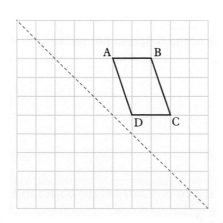

3

● 6

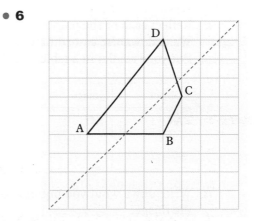

Exercise 2:3

1 a Copy the grid and the mirror line on to squared paper.

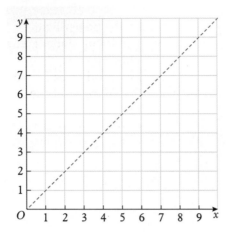

b Plot and label these points.
Join them up as you go along.
A (1, 1) $\longrightarrow$ B (2, 4) $\longrightarrow$ C (2, 3) $\longrightarrow$ D (4, 8) $\longrightarrow$
E (4, 6) $\longrightarrow$ F (6, 9) $\longrightarrow$ G (6, 8) $\longrightarrow$ H (8, 8)

c Reflect the shape you have drawn in the mirror line.
Label the image using the dash notation.

2 a Copy the grid and the mirror line from question **1**.
b Plot and label these object points.

A (2, 1)   C (1, 3)   E (7, 7)   G (8, 9)
B (4, 2)   D (6, 4)   F (3, 5)   H (3, 0)

c Reflect each of the points in the mirror line.
Write down the co-ordinates of each of the reflected points.
Put your results in a table like this.

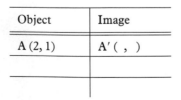

Object	Image
A (2, 1)	A' (,)

d Write down what you notice about the co-ordinates of the object and
the image.

2 Rotation

This is a theme park ride.
There is a lot of Maths going on
in a theme park!
The 'fun' in this ride is to be
rotated in more than one
direction.

| **Rotation** | A **rotation** turns a shape about a fixed point. |
| **Centre of rotation** | This fixed point is called the **centre of rotation**. |

As well as the centre of rotation, you need to know:
(1) the direction to turn (clockwise or anti-clockwise) and
(2) the angle that you turn through.

Example Describe the rotation from the red arrow to the blue arrow.

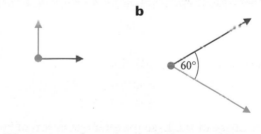

a The centre of rotation is the green spot.
The rotation is 90° anti-clockwise.
b The centre of rotation is the purple spot.
The rotation is 60° clockwise.

Exercise 2:4

1 Describe the rotation from the red arrow to the blue arrow.

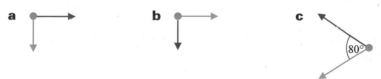

2 Describe the rotation from the red T-shape to the blue T-shape in each of these.

a

c

b

d

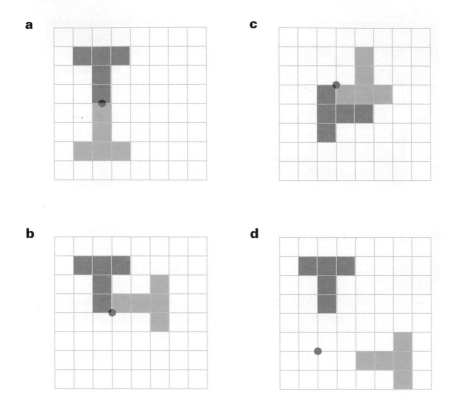

3 For each part:
(1) copy the diagram
(2) draw the image of the L-shape after a rotation of 90° clockwise about the green spot.

a

b

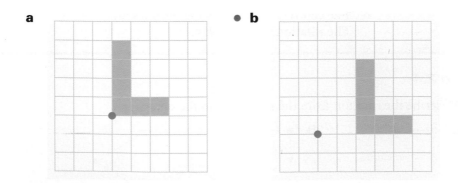

You might be able to draw rotations very easily.
Some people can see the answers on the page before they draw them.
If you can't, it is still very easy to draw them.
You can ask for tracing paper.

To rotate a shape about any point:

(1) Trace the shape in pencil.
(2) Lightly shade on the back of the tracing paper.
(3) Put your pencil on the centre of rotation and rotate the tracing paper through the angle that you need.
(4) Draw over the shape on your tracing paper with your book underneath.
(5) Remove the tracing paper and go over the shape which will have appeared on your page.

If you draw a cross at the centre of rotation it will help you to see when you have rotated through 90°, 180° and 270°.

Exercise 2:5

1 For each part:
   (1) copy the diagram
   (2) use tracing paper to rotate the shape about the green spot through the angle given.

a

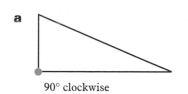

90° clockwise

b

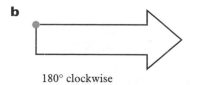

180° clockwise

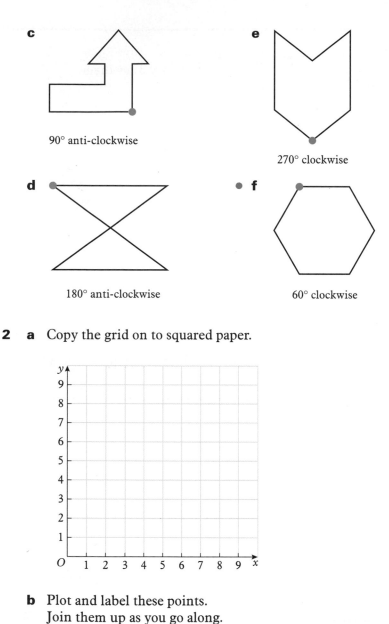

c

90° anti-clockwise

e

270° clockwise

d

180° anti-clockwise

f

60° clockwise

2 a Copy the grid on to squared paper.

b Plot and label these points.
Join them up as you go along.
A (1, 5)   B (2, 7)   C (4, 7)   D (4, 5)

c Rotate the shape you have drawn through 90° anti-clockwise about
the point (5, 5).
Label the image using the dash notation.

d Draw the line that goes through (0, 0), (1, 1), (2, 2), etc. on your
diagram.

e Reflect shape ABCD in the line you have drawn in **d**.

f What do you need to do to the shape you have drawn in **e** to
transform it to shape A′B′C′D′?

3 Number patterns

1 **Prime numbers**

2 **Polygon numbers**

Three is the first odd prime number

The natural world is three-dimensional

Three is a triangular number

Three is the smallest number of sides that a polygon can have

The world is traditionally divided into three parts: the underworld, the Earth and the heavens

Pi, one of the most famous numbers in maths, is a little more than 3. It is 3.141 592 6...

1 Prime numbers

Prime numbers have fascinated mathematicians for centuries.

There are many theorems and rules based on prime numbers. This section looks at some of them.

Prime numbers **Prime numbers** have only two factors, themselves and 1.
Some prime numbers are 2, 17, 19, 23.

9 is not a prime number because it is divisible by 3.
46 is not a prime number because it is divisible by 2 and 23.
1 is not a prime number because it does not have two factors.

Exercise 3:1

1 Write down all the prime numbers between 1 and 100.
You should have 25 altogether.

2 Twin primes are pairs of prime numbers that differ by two and have just one even number between them.
An example of twin primes is 3 and 5.
Find all the twin primes between 1 and 100.
Write them down in pairs.

3 Triple primes are sets of three prime numbers where the gap between each number in the triple is two bigger than the previous gap.
An example of a triple prime is 5, 7 and 11.
  a Find all the triple primes between 1 and 100.
  b What is the next triple above 100?

Exercise 3:2 Goldbach's Conjecture

Christian Goldbach lived from 1690 to 1764. He was a mathematician who did a lot of work on the theory of numbers and prime numbers in particular.
In 1742 he came up with his now famous conjecture.
A conjecture is a theory, which you believe to be true but cannot prove.

This is Goldbach's Conjecture. It is in two parts.
a Every even number greater than 4 is the sum of two odd prime numbers.
b Every odd number greater than 7 is the sum of three odd prime numbers.

1 You are going to look at the even numbers first.
Copy and complete this table. Leave space to add more rows.

Even number	Sum of two odd primes	Other solutions
6	3 + 3	
8	3 + 5	
10	3 + 7	5 + 5
12		
14		
16		
18		
20		

2 Add more rows to test Goldbach's Conjecture for even numbers up to 100.
You will see that some numbers have quite a few different solutions, 34 for example.
Try to find all the possibilities for each number.

3 You are now going to test the other half of the conjecture.
Copy and complete this table. Leave space to add more rows.

Odd number	Sum of three odd primes	Other solutions
9	3 + 3 + 3	
11	3 + 3 + 5	
13	3 + 5 + 5	3 + 3 + 7
15		
17		
19		
21		

4 Add more rows to test Goldbach's Conjecture for odd numbers up to 99.
Again, some numbers have quite a few solutions.
Try to find all the possibilities for each number.

Goldbach's Conjecture has been tested and found to be true for numbers
over 200 000 but it has never been proved. This means that
mathematicians can't be sure that it will work for **all** numbers.

To test if a number is prime, you need to divide the number by all prime numbers
between 2 and the square root of the number you are testing.
This is because a number can't have a prime factor bigger than its own square root,
except for itself.

Example

Is 113 a prime number?

First, find the square root of 113 on a calculator.

$\sqrt{113} = 10.63$ (to 2 decimal places)
This means that 113 has no prime factors bigger than 10.

Now, divide 113 by all the prime numbers between 2 and 10 in
turn. If any divide exactly then 113 is not prime.
$113 \div 2 = 56.5$
$113 \div 3 = 4.333\,333\,3\ldots$
$113 \div 5 = 22.6$
$113 \div 7 = 16.14$ (2 dp)

None of the numbers divide exactly into 113. This means that
113 is a prime number.

Exercise 3:3

1 a Find the square root of 117. Write it down correct to 2 dp.
b Write down all the prime numbers between 2 and your answer to **a**.
c Test 117 to see if it is prime.

2 **a** Find the square root of 227. Write it down correct to 2 dp.
b Write down all the prime numbers between 2 and your answer to **a**.
c Test 227 to see if it is prime.

3 Is 219 a prime number?

4 Test each of these numbers and decide whether or not it is prime.
a 337   **b** 261   **c** 783   **d** 1001

5 Test each of these numbers and decide whether or not it is prime.
a 997   **b** 10101   **c** 10301   **d** 7531

Exercise 3:4   Chebyshev's Theorem

Chebyshev was a Russian mathematician who lived from 1821 to 1894. He proved the following theorem. A theorem is a conjecture that has been proved.

Between every whole number greater than 1 and its double, there is at least one prime number.

Think about the number 4. Its double is 8 and between 4 and 8 are 5 and 7 which are both prime numbers.

Design a table to test Chebyshev's Theorem for numbers up to 100.

Lots of mathematicians have tried to find patterns in prime numbers.
They have also looked for rules and formulas to work them out.
This exercise looks at some of them.

Exercise 3:5

1 **a** Write down all the multiples of 6 between
6 and 96 in a column down the centre of
your page.
   b Write down all the numbers which are one
   less than the multiples of 6 in a column on
   the left hand side of your page.
   c Write down all the numbers which are one
   more than the multiples of 6 in a column on
   the right hand side of your page.
   d Circle all the prime numbers on the page.
   Are there any missing?
   e Investigate to see if this pattern continues beyond 100.

5	6	7
11	12	13
17	18	19
23	24	25
29	30	31
...	...	...
...	...	...

2 Copy this table. Fill in the blank spaces.

Starting number	1	2	3	4	5	6	7	8	9	10	11	12	13
Starting number squared	1	4	9	16	25								
Take away starting number	0	2	6	12	20								
Add 11	11	13	17	23	31								

   a What do you notice about the numbers in the bottom row?
   b Does the pattern continue if you start with numbers bigger than 13?

3 **a** Draw another table like the one in question **2**, but with 'Add 17' as
its last row.
   b Fill in your table.
   c Write down what you notice.
   d Repeat parts **a** to **c** but with 'Add 41' as the last instruction.

2 Polygon numbers

You have already seen square and triangular numbers.

You can also make up patterns from other polygons such as pentagons and hexagons.

Square numbers

1, 4, 9, 16, 25, ... are called **square numbers**.
Square numbers are found by multiplying a whole number by itself, so $1 \times 1 = 1$, $2 \times 2 = 4$ and $3 \times 3 = 9$
The numbers make square patterns.

Triangular numbers

1, 3, 6, 10, 15, 21, ... are called **triangular numbers**.
These numbers make triangular patterns.

Exercise 3:6

1 **a** Draw dot patterns for square numbers from 1 to 25.
   b Draw diagonal lines on your patterns like this:

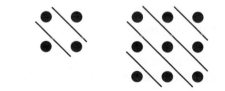

c Use your diagrams to explain this pattern.

1   = 1
1 + 2 + 1   = 4
1 + 2 + 3 + 2 + 1 = 9
etc.

2 a Draw another set of dot patterns for square numbers from 1 to 25.
  b Draw L shapes on your patterns like this:

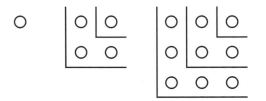

c Use your diagrams to explain this pattern.

1   = 1
1 + 3   = 4
1 + 3 + 5   = 9
etc.

3 a Draw another set of dot patterns for square numbers from 1 to 25.
  b Draw one diagonal line on your patterns just above the centre like this:

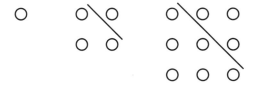

c Write down a number pattern from your diagrams.
  d Use your diagrams to explain why two consecutive triangular numbers make a square number.

4 a Copy this table of triangular numbers.

Number of pattern	1	2	3	4	5	6	7
Triangular number	1	3	6	10	15	21	28

  b Look at the **third** triangular number. Multiple 3 by 4. What do you have to do to the result of this calculation to get the third triangular number?
    Check if this method works for other triangular numbers in your table.
  c Write down a rule for working out the 10th triangular number.

You can work out sequences of numbers using other polygons.

Exercise 3:7

1 **a** Copy this diagram. You can trace it if you wish.

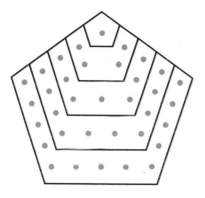

b The diagram shows pentagon numbers.
The first three are 1, 5 and 12.
Write down the next three pentagon numbers.

2 **a** Copy this diagram.

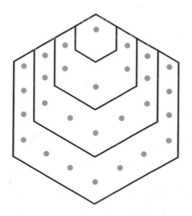

b The diagram shows hexagon numbers.
Write down the first six hexagon numbers.

3 Use these diagrams to write down the first six heptagonal and octagonal numbers.

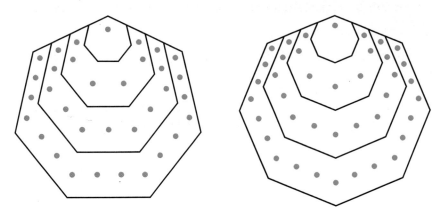

4 a Copy this table and fill it in using your answers to the previous questions.

Type of number	1st	2nd	3rd	4th	5th	6th
Triangular						
Square						
Pentagonal						
Hexagonal						
Heptagonal						
Octagonal						

   b Add together the fourth triangular number and the fifth square number.
   Which number in the table do you get?
   Does this work with other pairs of triangular and square numbers?

   c Add together the fifth triangular number and the sixth hexagonal number.
   Which number in the table do you get?
   Does this work with other pairs of triangular and hexagonal numbers?

   d Investigate other patterns like those in **b** and **c**.

5 a Try this method for working out the 4th hexagonal number.
   Multiply 4 by 2 and subtract 1. Multiply the result by 4.

   b Try this rule for other hexagonal numbers.

6 Work out a rule for octagonal numbers.

A trick with square numbers

It is possible to use square numbers to make some calculations easier.

Look at this simple statement: $3 \times 5 = 15$

The two numbers 3 and 5 have a difference of 2 and the number in the middle of them is 4.
$4^2 = 16$ which is one bigger than 15.
This suggests that **squaring the number in the middle** of 3 and 5 and **then subtracting 1** will give the correct answer to 3×5.

Exercise 3:8

1 Work out each of these using the method described above.
  a 5×7 **c** 7×9 **e** 10×12 **g** 16×18
  b 6×8 **d** 8×10 **f** 13×15 **h** 19×21

2 Look at the equation $3 \times 7 = 21$
  The difference between the numbers is 4 and the number in the middle is 5.
  Look for a rule similar to the one you used in question **1** to work this out.

3 Use the rule you found in question **2** to work out each of these.
  a 5×9 **c** 6×10 **e** 11×15 **g** 18×22
  b 4×8 **d** 8×12 **f** 13×17 **h** 96×100

4 It is possible to come up with similar rules for other differences.
  Copy this table. Fill it in.
  You will need to try out some rules.

To multiply two numbers that differ by ...	Square the number midway between the two then subtract ...
2	1
4	
6	
8	
10	

Exercise 3:9   Square chains

1   Choose any 2 digit number.

2   Square each digit of the number.

3   Add the two square numbers together.

4   Repeat steps 2 and 3 with your new number.

5   Draw a chain with your results at each stage.

> 53
>
> $5^2 = 25$ $3^2 = 9$
>
> $25 + 9 = 34$
>
> $3^2 = 9$ $4^2 = 16$
>
> $9 + 16 = 25$
>
> $53 \longrightarrow 34 \longrightarrow 25$

6   Continue the process until you realise that it is time to stop!
You may well need to redraw your chain at this point to make your results clearer.

7   Now pick another starting number and use the same process on it.
You will probably be able to link this new chain into your old one at some point.

8   Start with the number 32.
What happens? How can you show this on your diagram?

9   Write yourself out a list of all the numbers from 1 to 100 or get a number square.
Cross out all the numbers that are already on your diagram.
Now start with some of the numbers that haven't yet appeared.

10   When you have included all the numbers, draw out a new neat version of your diagram.

Powerful numbers

Four is a square number and the first square of a prime number

Einstein called time the fourth dimension

There are four points of the compass: north, south, east, west

The simplest platonic solid is the tetrahedron, which has four faces

One of the most famous problems in maths is the four-colour problem

1 Number puzzles

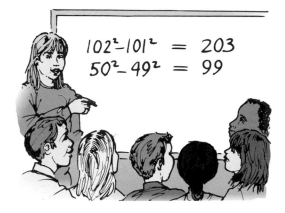

$102^2 - 101^2 = 203$
$50^2 - 49^2 = 99$

Jane is amazing her friends with her mental arithmetic. She has challenged them to work out these problems on their calculator faster than she can do them in her head. Each time they fail!
You use the properties of powers to do this trick.

Example   Look at these expressions. You could work out the value of both of them using your calculator.

a $23^2 - 22^2$ **b** $(23 + 22) \times (23 - 22)$

a Key in $\boxed{2}$ $\boxed{3}$ $\boxed{x^2}$ $\boxed{-}$ $\boxed{2}$ $\boxed{2}$ $\boxed{x^2}$ $\boxed{=}$

$23^2 - 22^2 = 45$

b Key in $\boxed{(}$ $\boxed{2}$ $\boxed{3}$ $\boxed{+}$ $\boxed{2}$ $\boxed{2}$ $\boxed{)}$ $\boxed{\times}$ $\boxed{(}$ $\boxed{2}$ $\boxed{3}$ $\boxed{-}$ $\boxed{2}$ $\boxed{2}$ $\boxed{)}$ $\boxed{=}$

$(23 + 22) \times (23 - 22) = 45$

Both expressions give the same answer but **b** is easy to do in your head.

$(23 + 22) \times (23 - 22) = 45 \times 1 = 45$

Exercise 4:1

1 a Copy this table. Fill in the missing values.

$12^2 - 11^2 = ...$	$(12 + 11) \times (12 - 11) = ... \times ... = ...$
$15^2 - 14^2 = ...$	$(15 + 14) \times (15 - 14) = ... \times ... = ...$
$32^2 - 31^2 = ...$	$(32 + 31) \times (32 - 31) = ... \times ... = ...$
$45^2 - 44^2 = ...$	$(45 + 44) \times (45 - 44) = ... \times ... = ...$
$50^2 - 49^2 = ...$	$(50 + 49) \times (50 - 49) = ... \times ... = ...$

b Look at the answers in each column. What do you notice?

c Look at the two numbers that are squared in the first column.
Now look at the numbers in the two brackets in the second column.
What do you notice?

d Write down the rule to work out these problems easily in
your head.

2 Use the rule that you found in question **1** to work these out in your
head:

a $13^2 - 12^2$	**d** $100^2 - 99^2$	**g** $93^2 - 92^2$
b $44^2 - 43^2$	**e** $60^2 - 59^2$	**h** $120^2 - 119^2$
c $30^2 - 29^2$	**f** $81^2 - 80^2$	**i** $150^2 - 149^2$

3 **a** Copy this table. Fill in the missing values.

$12^2 - 10^2 = \ldots$	$(12 + 10) \times (12 - 10) = \ldots \times \ldots = \ldots$
$15^2 - 13^2 = \ldots$	$(15 + 13) \times (15 - 13) = \ldots \times \ldots = \ldots$
$32^2 - 30^2 = \ldots$	$(32 + 30) \times (32 - 30) = \ldots \times \ldots = \ldots$
$43^2 - 41^2 = \ldots$	$(43 + 41) \times (43 - 41) = \ldots \times \ldots = \ldots$
$25^2 - 23^2 = \ldots$	$(25 + 23) \times (25 - 23) = \ldots \times \ldots = \ldots$

b Look at the first column.
How have the pairs of two squared numbers changed?

c How has the change in the first column affected the pattern in the
second column?

d Write down the rule to work out these problems easily in
your head.

4 Use the rule that you found in question **3** to work these out in
your head:

a $13^2 - 11^2$	**d** $101^2 - 99^2$	**g** $105^2 - 103^2$
b $44^2 - 42^2$	**e** $31^2 - 29^2$	**h** $112^2 - 110^2$
c $22^2 - 20^2$	**f** $81^2 - 79^2$	**i** $151^2 - 149^2$

5 Use the quick method to work out:

a $14^2 - 11^2$ **c** $18^2 - 12^2$ **e** $35^2 - 30^2$

b $41^2 - 39^2$ **d** $24^2 - 14^2$ **f** $15^2 - 11^2$

6 Work these out in your head. You can now amaze your friends!

a $22^2 - 19^2$ **d** $73^2 - 68^2$ **g** $120^2 - 110^2$

b $44^2 - 34^2$ **e** $31^2 - 11^2$ **h** $181^2 - 179^2$

c $22^2 - 18^2$ **f** $42^2 - 22^2$ **i** $151^2 - 141^2$

You can use the $\boxed{x^y}$ key on your calculator to work out powers of numbers.

Example   Work out the value of   **a** $4^2 - 2^3$ **b** $5 \times (3^4 - 2^5)$

To work out 2^3 you key in $\boxed{2}$ $\boxed{x^y}$ $\boxed{3}$ $\boxed{=}$

a $4^2 - 2^3 = 16 - 8$

            $= 8$

b $5 \times (3^4 - 2^5) = 5 \times (81 - 32)$

                     $= 5 \times 49$

                     $= 245$

Exercise 4:2

Work out the value of these:

1 $3^4 + 5^2$ **5** $(8^2 - 2^5) \times (10 - 3^2)$

2 $7^2 - 3^3$ **6** $(6^2 + 4) \div (3^2 - 1)$

3 $(5^3 - 6^2) \times 2$ **7** $(5^3 - 2^4) \times 10^3$

4 $2^2 + 3^2 + 3^2$ **8** $100 \div 5^2 + 2^8$

9 Copy the table. Fill it in.

Power	Number	International name	American name
10^2	100	hundred	hundred
10^3		thousand	thousand
10^6		million	million
10^9		milliard	billion
10^{12}		billion	trillion
10^{15}		—	quadrillion
10^{18}		trillion	quintillion
10^{100}	1 followed by 100 zeros	googol	googol

Carol's Maths teacher has given her this problem.
She has to use the digits 2, 2, 3, 4, 5 to get an
answer equal to 29.
Each digit can only be used once.
All digits must be used.
The solution must contain at least one power.

First try: $3^2 + 4^2 + 5 = 30$

Second try: $5^2 - 4^2 + 3 = 12$

Third try: $2^3 + 5^2 - 4 = 29$ ✓

Exercise 4:3

For each question you are given a set of digits and the required answer.
Use the same rules as Carol to find the solution.

1 1, 2, 4, 7   46

2 2, 2, 3, 3   31

3 2, 2, 4, 5   42

4 1, 2, 3, 4, 5   3

5 2, 2, 2, 2, 3, 4   29

6 2, 3, 4, 5, 9   100

7 2, 2, 2, 3, 5   9

8 2, 2, 2, 2, 2, 3, 5, 6   55

2 Graphs of powers

Peter is on holiday with his family. His dad wants him to fetch the paper each day from the local shop. He offers to pay him 2 p the first day, 4 p the second day, 8 p the third day, and so on.

The family is on holiday for three weeks. Peter does not want to do it.

His granny is a mathematician. She tells Peter that he could make a lot of money, but he does not believe her. How much would Peter make?

Exercise 4:4

1 a Copy this table.

The 1st day Peter gets	2 pence
The 2nd day Peter gets	$2 \times 2 = 2^2 =$ 4 pence
The 3rd day Peter gets	$2 \times 2 \times 2 = 2^3 =$ 8 pence
The 4th day Peter gets	$2 \times 2 \times 2 \times 2 = 2^4 = 16$ pence

b Write in the next three lines of the table.
c Add up the amounts for each of the 7 days to find out how much Peter gets in total for the first week.

2 a On the 14th day Peter gets 2^{14} pence.
   Use your calculator to work out how much Peter gets on the 14th day.
b How much would Peter get in total if the holiday lasted 2 weeks?
c How much would Peter get on the 21st day?
d How much, in £, would he get in total for the three week holiday?

3 Peter negotiates to be paid 3 p on the 1st day and each day the amount is multiplied by 3.
a Draw a table showing how much he gets for each of the first 5 days.
b Find the total amount, in £, that Peter will get for a holiday lasting:
   (1) 1 week   (2) 2 weeks   (3) 3 weeks.

4 Peter's granny decides to plot a graph to show Peter what is happening.

a She draws this table showing the amount for each of the first 6 days. Copy the table. Fill it in.

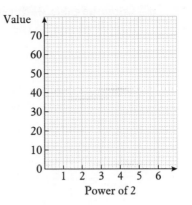

Value

Power of 2

	Power	Value
2^1	1	2
2^2	2	4
2^3	3	8
2^4	...	...
2^5	...	...
2^6	...	...

b Copy the axes on to squared paper.

c Plot the powers of 2 against their values.
The points to plot are:
(1, 2) (2, 4) (3, 8) and so on.

d Join the points with a curve.
Your curve should look like this.

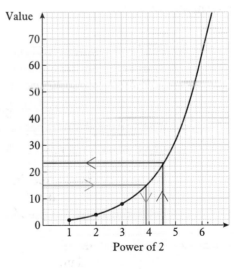

Value

Power of 2

e Use your graph to find the value of $2^{4.5}$
Draw the red line on your graph.
Start at 4.5 on the horizontal axis.
Draw a vertical line to the curve then a horizontal line to the vertical axis.
Read off the value of $2^{4.5}$

f Use your graph to find the value of $2^{5.5}$

g What power of 2 does 15 equal?
Draw the blue line on your graph.
Start at 15 on the vertical axis, draw across to the curve then down to the horizontal axis.
Read off the value of the power.

h Copy these.

$$2^{...} = 40 \qquad 2^{...} = 28$$

Use your graph to fill in the missing powers.

5 **a** Copy the table. Fill it in.
Square means 'to the power 2'
so 5 squared $= 5^2$

Number	Square
1	1
2	4
3	9
4	16
5	...
6	...
7	...
8	...

b Copy the axes on to graph paper.

c Plot the squares against the numbers.
The points to plot are:

(1, 1) (2, 4) (3, 9) and so on.

d Join the points with a curve.

e Use your graph to find the square of 3.5
Start at 3.5 on the horizontal axis. Draw a vertical line to the curve then a horizontal line to the vertical axis.
Read off the square of 3.5

f The square of a number is 22. Use your graph to find the number.

g Copy these.
Use your graph to fill in the missing numbers.
$2.6^2 = ...$ $...^2 = 28$

Square root

Square root undoes a square. It returns you to the number that you started with.

6 squared $= 36$ the square root of $36 = 6$
You have returned to 6

6 squared is written 6^2
The square root of 36 is written $\sqrt{36}$

'Square root' is the inverse of 'square'.

---

6 Write down the value of each of these:
    a 11 squared   **c** 35^2 **e** $\sqrt{144}$
    b the square root of 100   **d** $\sqrt{49}$ **f** the square of 3

Cube root

Cube means 'to the power 3' so 2 cubed $- 2^3 - 2 \times 2 \times 2 = 8$
Cube root undoes a cube.

9 cubed $= 729$ the cube root of $729 = 9$

9 cubed is written 9^3 the cube root of 729 is written $\sqrt[3]{729}$

'Cube root' is the inverse of 'cube'.

---

7 Write down the value of each of these:
    a 4 cubed   **c** 6^3 **e** $\sqrt[3]{125}$
    b the cube root of 8   **d** $\sqrt[3]{1000}$ **f** the cube of 12

You can use a calculator to work out roots.

The square root key is marked $\sqrt{}$

The cube root key is marked $\sqrt[3]{}$

To find $\sqrt{16}$ key in

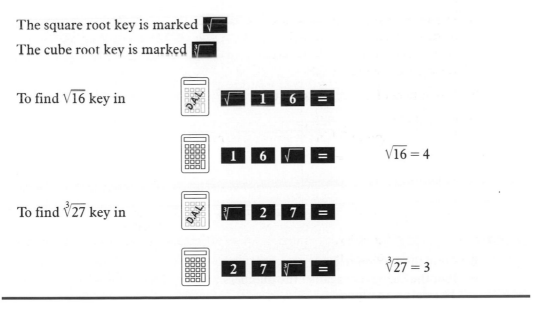

$\sqrt{16} = 4$

To find $\sqrt[3]{27}$ key in

$\sqrt[3]{27} = 3$

---

8 Use your calculator to find the value of:
    a 4^6 **c** $\sqrt[3]{1331}$ **e** 2^{11} **g** $\sqrt[3]{343}$
    b $\sqrt{289}$ **d** 3^4 **f** $\sqrt[3]{64}$ **h** $\sqrt{361}$

9 **a** Copy the table. Fill it in.

Number	Square root
16	4
36	6
49	7
81	
100	
121	

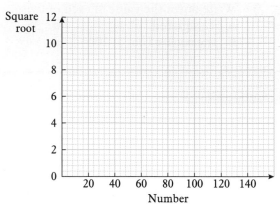

b Copy the axes on to graph paper.
c Plot the square roots against the numbers.
   The points to plot are:
   (16, 4) (36, 6) (49, 7) and so on.
d Join the points with a curve.
e Use your graph to find the square root of 60.
f The square root of a number is 8.3 Use your graph to find the number.

10 **a** Copy the table. Fill it in.

Number	Cube root
8	2
27	3
64	
125	
216	

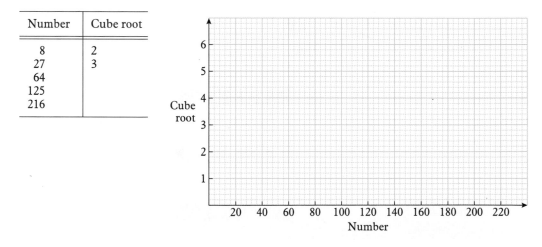

b Copy the axes on to graph paper.
c Plot the cube roots against the numbers.
   The points to plot are:
   (8, 2) (27, 3) (64, ...) and so on.
d Join the points with a curve.
e Use your graph to find the cube root of 100.
f The cube root of a number is 4.7
   Use your graph to find the number.

5 Shape and construction

1 **Angles in polygons**

2 **Escher pictures**

Five is the smallest number which is the sum of two different square numbers

There are five platonic solids. These are solids whose faces are all regular polygons

Five is the first prime number which is one less than a multiple of six

The Romans used V to represent five

Five is the fifth number of the Fibonacci sequence

1 Angles in polygons

This is a picture of a Roman wall.
The Romans used lots of small tiles and made patterns in the wall by joining the tiles together.
The small tiles were called tessellae.

This is where the word tessellation comes from.

In this section you are going to see which polygons will tessellate.

| Angle at a point | The **angle at a point** is 360°.
This is the angle in a full turn.

Exercise 5:1

1 Here is a tessellation made from equilateral triangles.

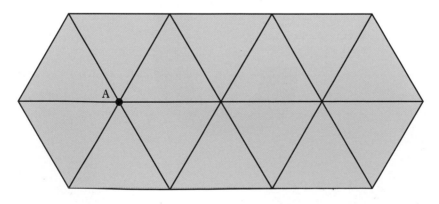

a How many equilateral triangles meet at point A?
b Write down the angle at A.
c What is the angle at each vertex of an equilateral triangle?

2 **a** Draw a tessellation of squares.
  b How many squares are there at each point where the squares meet?
  c What is the angle at each vertex of a square?

Regular tessellation   **A regular tessellation** is a tessellation that is made from one regular polygon.

The tessellations that you have seen so far are regular tessellations.

▼ You need Worksheet 5:1 for the rest of this exercise.

3 For each of the regular polygons:
  a Try to draw a regular tessellation.
  b If you can draw a regular tessellation, work out the angle at each vertex of the polygon.
  c Put your results in a table like this:

Polygon	Regular tessellation ✓ or ✗	Angle at each vertex
equilateral triangle	✓	...°
square	...	...°

Semi-regular tessellation   A **semi-regular tessellation** is a tessellation made from two regular polygons.

This is a semi-regular tessellation made from regular hexagons and equilateral triangles.

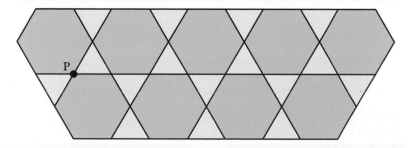

You can find angles using semi-regular tessellations.

In this tessellation two equilateral triangles and two
hexagons meet at each point like P in the tessellation.

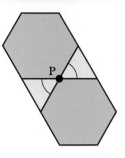

The angle at P is 360°.
You know that the angle in an equilateral triangle is 60°.
There are two of these angles at P.
So there are 120° in the triangles.
This leaves 240° for the two hexagons.
So the angle at each vertex of a regular hexagon is 120°.

You should already know this from your previous work
but it gives you another way to find the angles in regular polygons.

4 You can draw a semi-regular tessellation using octagons and squares.

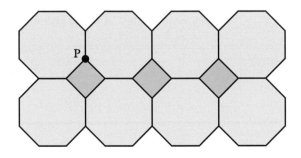

a How many of each polygon meet at P?
b What is the angle at each vertex of a regular octagon?

5 Find as many semi-regular tessellations as you can.
Draw all the semi-regular tessellations that you find.
Mark all the angles in the polygons at one of the points of each
tessellation and show that they add up to 360°.
Check to see if you can find the angle at each vertex of any more regular
polygons.

| Interior angle | The **interior angle** of a regular polygon is the angle inside the polygon at each vertex. |

Exercise 5:2

1 Copy this table. Fill in as much as you can using your answers from the last exercise.

Regular polygon	Interior angle
triangle	
square	
pentagon	
hexagon	
heptagon	
octagon	

To find the missing angles in your table, you need to have a different way of working out the angles.

| Angles in a triangle | The **angles in a triangle** add up to 180°. In an equilateral triangle all the angles are equal. So each angle is 180° ÷ 3 = 60° |

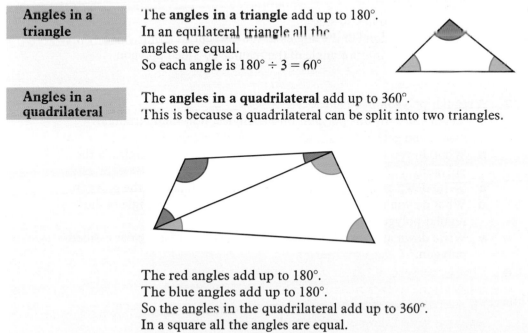

| Angles in a quadrilateral | The **angles in a quadrilateral** add up to 360°. This is because a quadrilateral can be split into two triangles. |

The red angles add up to 180°.
The blue angles add up to 180°.
So the angles in the quadrilateral add up to 360°.
In a square all the angles are equal.
So each angle = 360° ÷ 4 = 90°

2 **a** Draw a pentagon.
   b Split the pentagon into triangles starting from one vertex.
   c Work out the total of the angles in a pentagon.
   d Work out the interior angle of a regular pentagon.

3 **a** Draw a hexagon.
   b Split the hexagon into triangles starting from one vertex.
   c Work out the total of the angles in a hexagon.
   d Work out the interior angle of a regular hexagon.
       Check that it is the same as in your table from question **1**.

4 Work out the interior angle in each of the remaining polygons in your
   table from question **1**.
   Put your answers into the table.

5 **a** Draw a decagon.
   b Split the decagon into triangles starting from one vertex.
   c Work out the total of the angles in a decagon.
   d Work out the interior angle of a regular decagon.

6 A regular polygon has 20 sides.
   a Work out the total of the angles in the polygon.
   b Work out the interior angle of the regular 20-sided polygon.

7 A regular polygon has n sides.
   a When you split this polygon into triangles, how many triangles
       would you get?
   b What do you do to this number to get the total of the angles in the
       polygon?
   c Write down an expression for the total of the angles in the polygon.
   d What do you do to this total to work out the interior angle of the
       regular polygon?
   e Write down an expression for the interior angle of a regular n-sided
       polygon.

2 Escher pictures

This is a picture by the famous Dutch artist M C Escher.

Escher used his knowledge of tessellations to help with his designs.

The first fact that Escher used is that every quadrilateral will tessellate.
Some tessellate with all of the shapes exactly the same way up

and some have to be turned over

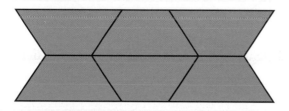

but all of them will tessellate.

Exercise 5:3

1 Draw a tessellation of:
   a a parallelogram   **b** a kite.

2 Will all triangles tessellate?
   Explain your answer.

The next fact that Escher used is that if you start with any quadrilateral and cut a piece out of it and move it to the opposite side, the shape you get will still tessellate.

Start with a rectangle.

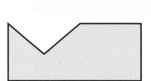

Cut out a V shape from the top

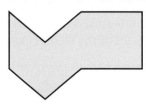

and move it to the bottom like this.

This new shape will still tessellate.

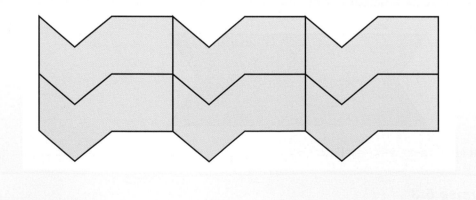

3 Draw your own tessellations like the one above.
Cut out different shapes from a rectangle.

Now all you need to do is let your imagination run away with you!
You can do this with any shape that tessellates and you can cut out more than
one piece.
You don't have to cut out straight edges either.

Start with a rectangle again.

Cut out a semi-circle from the top
and put it on the bottom like this.

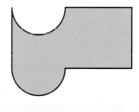

Now cut out and move another
piece like this

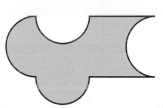

and this shape still tessellates!

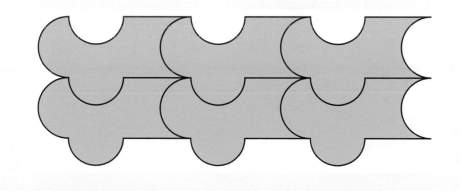

4 Draw your own tessellations like the one above. Cut out different shapes
from any shape that tessellates.

Finally Escher spotted that it does not just have to be movement from one side to the other. When you cut a piece out you can rotate through 180° too.

(1) Start with a rectangle again.

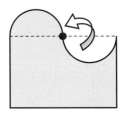

(2) Cut out a semi-circle from the top and rotate it like this.

(3) Now do the same on the bottom.

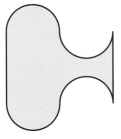

(4) Just one more step to get a fish!

The fishes tessellate too if you turn some of them over!

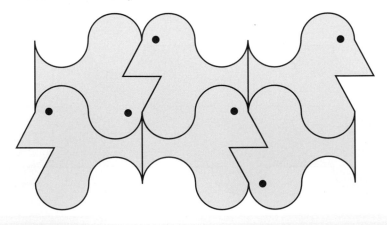

5 Draw your own tessellations like the one above.
Cut out and rotate different shapes from any shape that tessellates.
You can combine both the methods in this section to get even more amazing pictures.

6 Decimals and number bases

1 Decimals

2 Number bases

Six is the first perfect number

Six is a triangular number and the only triangular number with less than 660 digits whose square is also a triangular number

Six is the area of the first Pythagorean triangle

1, 2 and 3 are the only set of three integers where each number is a factor of the sum of the other two

1 Decimals

When you buy a new carpet, the cost depends on the area of the room you are carpeting.

Working out the area of a room often involves multiplying decimals together.

Multiplying decimals

Exercise 6:1

1 Copy this number pattern. Fill in the gaps.

$$4 \times 3 = 12$$
$$40 \times 3 = 120$$
$$40 \times 30 = 1200$$
$$400 \times 30 =$$
$$400 \times 300 =$$
$$4000 \times 300 =$$
$$4000 \times 3000 =$$

2 Copy this number pattern. Fill in the gaps.

$$6 \times 7 = 42$$
$$60 \times 7 = 420$$
$$60 \times 70 = 4200$$
$$600 \times 70 =$$
$$600 \times 700 =$$
$$6000 \times 700 =$$
$$6000 \times 7000 =$$

3 Work out the answers to these.

a 0.5×3 **b** 0.6×6 **c** 0.8×5 **d** 0.9×7

For question **3**, you should have the following answers:

a $0.5 \times 3 = 1.5$ **c** $0.8 \times 5 = 4.0$

b $0.6 \times 6 = 3.6$ **d** $0.9 \times 7 = 6.3$

Now think about the answer to the question **0.5 × 0.3**

You might have been tempted to say 1.5, but you have just seen that $0.5 \times 3 = 1.5$
0.5×0.3 can't give the same answer.

In fact, $0.5 \times 0.3 = 0.15$ Check it on a calculator.

Multiplying by 0.5 is the same as halving something.
This means that 0.5×0.3 is the same as working out half of 0.3
Half of 0.3 is 0.15, so the answer is sensible!

4 Copy the following questions and fill in the answers.
When you have done them all, check them on your calculator.

a 0.5×0.2 **c** 0.6×0.4 **e** 0.5×0.7

b 0.9×0.4 **d** 0.7×0.4 **f** 0.9×0.6

You may have noticed that when you multiply two decimals together

$0.6 \times 0.7 = 0.42$

there are two digits after the decimal points in the question (shown in red) and there are also two digits after the decimal point in the answer (shown in blue).

This will always happen provided that none of the decimals have 0s on the end. Any numbers that have, like 0.40, should be written as 0.4 *before* you count the number of decimal places.

Example   Work out   **a** 0.04×0.05 **b** 0.08×0.0006

a 0.04×0.05
Ignoring all the zeros, $4 \times 5 = 20$ and there are 4 digits after the decimal points. This means that the answer is 0.0020

b 0.08×0.0006
Ignoring all the zeros, $8 \times 6 = 48$ and there are 6 digits after the decimal points. This means that the answer is 0.000 048

Exercise 6:2

Write down the answers to each of these questions.

1 **a** 0.05×0.2 **d** 0.7×0.06
     b 0.09×0.3 **e** 0.05×0.03
     c 0.9×0.04 **f** 0.01×0.01

2 **a** 0.007×0.05 **d** 0.007×0.009
     b 0.006×0.003 **e** 0.0005×0.0003
     c 0.09×0.005 **f** 0.0003×0.00005

3 **a** 0.007×5 **d** 0.00008×0.00001
     b 0.000006×0.3 **e** 0.0005×30
     c 0.00009×0.000007 **f** 0.0007×0.0000007

4 **a** 0.003×0.015 **d** 0.07×0.0025
     b 0.006×0.0021 **e** 0.0035×0.0007
     c 0.04×0.032 **f** 0.00027×0.00027

Dividing decimals

When you **multiply** two decimals you have to **add** the number of decimal places in the two numbers to find the number of decimal places in the answer.

So, when you **divide** two decimals you have to **subtract** the number of decimal places in the two numbers to find the number of decimal places in the answer.

Example   Work out   **a** $0.00004 \div 0.02$ **b** $0.008 \div 0.002$

    a $0.00004 \div 0.02$
       Ignoring all the zeros, $4 \div 2 = 2$. There are 5 digits after the decimal point in the first number and 2 in the second.
       $5 - 2 = 3$ so there will be 3 digits after the decimal point in the answer.
       This means that the answer is 0.002

    b $0.008 \div 0.002$
       Ignoring all the zeros, $8 \div 2 = 4$. There are 3 digits after the decimal point in the first number and 3 in the second.
       $3 - 3 = 0$ so there will be no digits after the decimal point in the answer.
       This means that the answer is 4.

Exercise 6:3

Write down the answers to each of these questions.

1 **a** $0.06 \div 0.2$
 b $0.09 \div 0.3$
 c $0.09 \div 0.01$

   d $0.004 \div 0.02$
   e $0.09 \div 0.03$
   f $0.01 \div 0.01$

2 **a** $0.008 \div 0.04$
 b $0.006 \div 0.003$
 c $0.0009 \div 0.003$

   d $0.009 \div 0.001$
   e $0.0006 \div 0.0002$
   f $0.000\,008 \div 0.002$

3 **a** $0.007 \div 0.01$
 b $0.000\,006 \div 0.3$
 c $0.000\,09 \div 0.0003$

   d $0.000\,08 \div 0.000\,01$
   e $0.0006 \div 30$
   f $0.000\,000\,7 \div 0.0007$

4 **a** $0.0007 \div 0.02$
 b $0.0009 \div 0.002$
 c $0.005 \div 0.02$

   d $0.0005 \div 0.004$
   e $0.000\,03 \div 0.002$
   f $0.000\,27 \div 0.0002$

5 Something to think about!
How would you use the division rule on a calculation like
$0.5 \div 0.000\,02$?
There is 1 digit after the decimal point in the first number and 5 in the second number. What is $1 - 5$ and how do you use it to work out the answer to the question?

2 Number bases

When computers were first invented, it was discovered that they could not be made to count in tens like we do. They could only count in twos.

This system is known as binary. Modern computers still use binary numbers. In this section you are going to find out how binary numbers work.

When we write numbers, we write them in columns.
As you move from right to left, each column is ten times bigger than the previous one. We count in tens because we have 10 fingers. Early humans developed this system because they found it the easiest way to count. This system is called **base 10**.

For example:

thousands	hundreds	tens	units
1000s	100s	10s	1s
9	5	4	2

So in our number system the number 9542 means

$9 \times 1000 = 9000$
$5 \times 100 = 500$
$4 \times 10 = 40$
$2 \times 1 = 2$

When you use binary numbers, each column is 2 times bigger than the previous one as you go from right to left. Every time you get to 2 you carry into the next column. This means that you never write the number 2 in one column, just as we never write the number 10 in a single column. In binary, you only write the digits 1 and 0.
Binary is also called **base 2**.

The columns look like this:

sixty-fours	thirty-twos	sixteens	eights	fours	twos	units
64s	32s	16s	8s	4s	2s	1s

Exercise 6:4

1 Copy this table. Go up to 32 in the first column.

Number in base 10	thirty-twos	sixteens	eights	fours	twos	units
	32s	16s	8s	4s	2s	1s
1						
2						
3						
4						
5						
6						
7						

2 The number 1 is written the same as normal so put a 1 in the 1s column.

fours	twos	units
4s	2s	1s
		1

Write this in your table.

3 The number 2 is written like this:

fours	twos	units
4s	2s	1s
	1	0

It is made up of 1 lot of 2 and no units.
Write this in your table.

4 The number 3 is written like this:

fours	twos	units
4s	2s	1s
	1	1

It is made up of 1 lot of 2 and 1 unit.
Write this in your table.

5 Write the binary version of 4 in your table.

You should have put the number 100 in your table to represent 4.

6 5 is made up of 1 lot of 4 and 1 unit.
It is written 101 in binary.
Write this in your table.

7 Write the binary versions of 6 to 15 in your table.
Look for patterns as you enter the numbers in the table.

8 Fill in the rest of your table up to 32.

You can change binary numbers back into base 10 very easily.

Example Change the binary number 10011 to base 10.

First, write in the column headings.

sixteens	eights	fours	twos	units
16s	8s	4s	2s	1s
1	0	0	1	1

You can now see that this number is made up of 1 sixteen, 1 two and 1 unit.

Adding these together, $16 + 2 + 1 = 19$

So 10011 in binary is the same as 19 in base 10.

Exercise 6:5

1 Change the binary number 10101 into base 10.

2 Change the binary number 11001 into base 10.

3 Change the following binary numbers into base 10.
   a 10111   **c** 101010   **e** 1100101
   b 111   **d** 11011   **f** 111111

4 Change the following binary numbers into base 10.
   a 111111   **c** 11101010   **e** 110101010
   b 11101101   **d** 100011101   **f** 10100010101

You can also change base 10 numbers into binary.
To do this you keep dividing by 2.
This involves dividing the base 10 number by 2 and noting down the remainder
over and over again until you reach 0.

Example   Convert the number 87 into binary.

The division is set out vertically.

```
        remainder
2|8 7
  4 3   1      87 ÷ 2 = 43 remainder 1
  2 1   1      43 ÷ 2 = 21 remainder 1
  1 0   1      21 ÷ 2 = 10 remainder 1
    5   0      10 ÷ 2 =  5 remainder 0
    2   1       5 ÷ 2 =  2 remainder 1
    1   0       2 ÷ 2 =  1 remainder 0
    0   1       1 ÷ 2 =  0 remainder 1
```

To get the binary version of the number you now write down the
remainders starting at the **bottom**.
87 in base 10 is the same as 1 0 1 0 1 1 1 in binary.

Exercise 6:6

1   Change the base 10 number 54 into binary.

2   Change the base 10 number 73 into binary.

3   Change the following base 10 numbers into binary.
   a 23   **c** 91   **e** 121
   b 64   **d** 100   **f** 139

4   Change the following base 10 numbers into binary.
   a 200   **c** 256   **e** 511
   b 300   **d** 427   **f** 10 000

You can do all the usual operations like addition and subtraction on binary numbers.
Remember that you are only counting in 2s now instead of 10s.

Addition

Example

Work out 1010 + 1111 in binary.

Set the sum out like a normal addition.
Add up each column starting with the units.
Remember that if you get to two you need to carry into the next column.

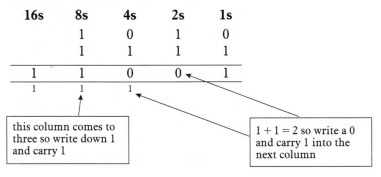

16s	8s	4s	2s	1s
	1	0	1	0
	1	1	1	1
1	1	0	0	1
1	1	1		

this column comes to three so write down 1 and carry 1

1 + 1 = 2 so write a 0 and carry 1 into the next column

1010 + 1111 = 11001

Exercise 6:7

1 Work out 101 + 101 in binary.

2 Work out 111 + 100 in binary.

3 Do the following binary additions.
   a 1010 + 111   **c** 1100 + 1001   **e** 10101 + 111
   b 1100 + 101   **d** 1011 + 1010   **f** 10011 + 1001

4 Do the following binary additions.
   a 11010 + 11010   **c** 11111 + 11111
   b 11101 + 1111   **d** 10101 + 101010

5 Convert the numbers in question **4** and your answers to base 10 to check that they are correct.

Subtraction

The main difference between binary subtraction and base 10 subtraction comes when you borrow. In base 10, when you can't do a subtraction in a column, you borrow 10 from the column on the left. In binary you borrow 2 instead of 10.

Example

Work out $1100 - 110$ in binary.

Set the sum out like a normal subtraction.
Subtract each column starting with the units.
Remember that if you can't do a subtraction in a column you need to borrow 2 from the next column on the left.

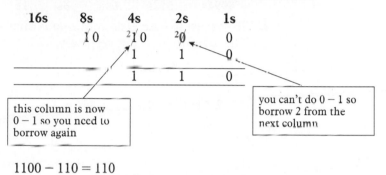

this column is now $0 - 1$ so you need to borrow again

you can't do $0 - 1$ so borrow 2 from the next column

$$1100 - 110 = 110$$

Exercise 6:8

1   Work out $1111 - 101$ in binary.

2   Work out $1110 - 110$ in binary.

3   Do the following binary subtractions.
  a $1010 - 111$ **c** $1100 - 1001$ **e** $10101 - 111$
  b $1100 - 101$ **d** $1011 - 1010$ **f** $10011 - 1001$

4   Do the following binary subtractions.
  a $11010 - 11010$ **c** $100001 - 11111$
  b $11101 - 1111$ **d** $1010101 - 101010$

5   Convert the numbers in question **4** and your answers to base 10 to check that they are correct.

Other bases

When you use binary numbers you are counting in twos.
You can use any number as a base.
You use the base number to work out the columns you need.

Example

a Work out the column headings for base 8 (octal).
b Write the base 10 number 176 in base 8.

a These are the column headings for base 8.
Each column is 8 times bigger than the one to the right of it.
4096s   512s   64s   8s   1s

b To convert to base 8, do continuous division by 8.
The division is set out vertically.

```
                    remainder
    8 | 1 7 6
        2 2        0        176 ÷ 8 = 22 remainder 0
          2        6         22 ÷ 8 =  2 remainder 6
          0        2          2 ÷ 8 =  0 remainder 2
```

To get the base 8 version of the number you now write down
the reminders starting at the **bottom**.
176 is the same as 260 in base 8.

Exercise 6:9

1 **a** Change the base 10 number 227 into base 8.
  b Change the base 10 number 4200 into base 8.

2 **a** Change the base 8 number 634 into base 10.
  b Change the base 8 number 2547 into base 10.

3 Do the following base 8 additions. Remember that every time you reach 8
or more you will have to carry into the next column.
  a $272 + 54$ **b** $651 + 245$ **c** $1234 + 7654$

4 Work out $605 - 257$ in base 8. Remember you will have to borrow 8s.

Exercise 6:10

1 **a** Work out the column headings for base 6 (senary).
    b Which digits in base 10 (0, 1, 2, 3, 4, 5, 6, 7, 8, 9) can you use in base 6?
    c Change the base 6 number 543 into base 10.
    d Change the base 10 number 872 into base 6.
    e Work out 453 + 325 in base 6.
    f Work out 534 − 255 in base 6.

2 **a** Work out the column headings for base 4 (quaternary).
    b Which digits in base 10 can you use in base 4?
    c Change the base 4 number 312 into base 10.
    d Change the base 10 number 358 into base 4.
    e Work out 231 + 223 in base 4.
    f Work out 301 − 133 in base 4.

3 **a** Work out the column headings for base 9 (nonary).
    b Change the base 9 number 487 into base 10.
    c Change the base 10 number 1000 into base 9.
    d Work out 782 + 625 in base 9.
    e Work out 400 − 188 in base 9.

4 Do each of the following calculations.
    Think carefully about the base before you start each one.

    a   563
        +247 (base 8)

    b   245
        −155 (base 6)

    c   876
        +888 (base 9)

5 Change 325 in base 6 into base 5.

6 Write the base 10 number 100 in each base from 2 to 9.
    Write about anything you notice about your answers.

7 Experiment to find a way to work out, in base 2, 11101 × 1101.
    You could change the numbers to base 10 to check your answers.
    The answer should be 101111001.

Hexadecimal

Hexadecimal is the name given to base 16.
You may be surprised to see a base bigger than 10, but it is possible.
In fact, hexadecimal (or just 'hex' for short!) is used a lot in computing.

Working in base 16 means that you do not have to carry into the next column until you have counted up to 16. This means that you need a single symbol to represent the base 10 numbers 10, 11, 12, 13, 14 and 15.
With little imagination, we use
A = 10, B = 11, C = 12, D = 13, E = 14 and F = 15

The columns in hex are: **4096s   256s   16s   1s**

Example   Convert the hex number 5A1 into base 10.

Write in the column headings: **256s   16s   1s**
                                    5   A   1

5 × 256 = 1280
10 × 16 = 160
1 × 1 = 1

So 5A1 in hex is 1280 + 160 + 1 = 1441 in base 10.

Exercise 6:11

1 **a** Change the hex number B7 into base 10.
    b Change the hex number 7FA into base 10.

2 **a** Change the base 10 number 227 into hex.
    b Change the base 10 number 4200 into hex.

3 Do these hex additions. Remember that you do not have to carry into the next column until you reach 16 or more.
    a 65 + 27   **b** 356 + 284   **c** 2A4 + 58E

4 Convert the binary number 111111111111 into hex.
    Write down anything you notice.

7 3-D: the extra dimension

1 **Surface area**

2 **Volume and solids**

There are seven days in a week

The fifty and twenty pence coins have seven sides

Seven is the fourth prime number

At least seven rectangles are needed if a rectangle is to be divided into smaller rectangles, none of which will fit inside another

Seven is the basis for the rhyme 'When I was going to St Ives ...'

1 Surface area

This packaging company produces thousands and thousands of boxes.
They want to make them in the most efficient way possible.
This means using as little card as possible. They want each box to have the smallest possible surface area.

Surface area   The **surface area** of a solid is the same as the area of its net.

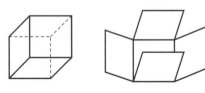
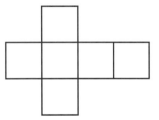

The surface area of this cube is the same as the area of this net.

To find the surface area of a solid shape, you can imagine opening up the solid and looking at its net. You then find the surface area of the net.

Exercise 7:1

1 **a** Draw an accurate net of this cube on squared paper.

   b Find the area of one of the squares of the net. Write your answer in cm² on the net.

   c Find the area of the whole net.

   d Write down the surface area of the cube.

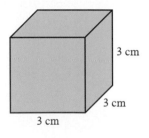

3 cm
3 cm
3 cm

2 For each cuboid in this question:

(1) Draw an accurate net of the cuboid on squared paper.

(2) Write the area of each of the six rectangles on the net.

(3) Find the area of the whole net.

(4) Write down the surface area of the cuboid.

a
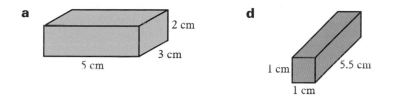

d

b
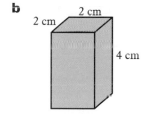

e
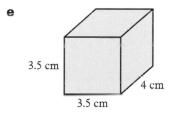

c

f
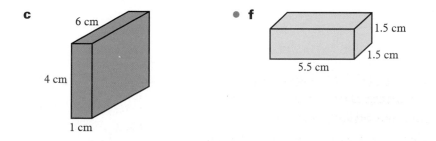

3 Find the surface area of each of these cuboids.

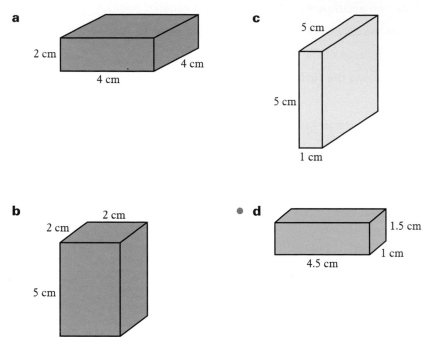

a

2 cm
4 cm
4 cm

c

5 cm
5 cm
1 cm

b

2 cm
2 cm
5 cm

d

1.5 cm
1 cm
4.5 cm

4 These four boxes all have the same amount of space inside them.
List the boxes in order of their surface area. Start with the smallest.

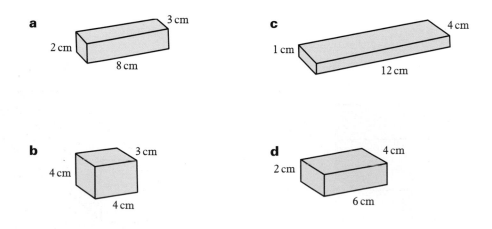

a

3 cm
2 cm
8 cm

c

4 cm
1 cm
12 cm

b

3 cm
4 cm
4 cm

d

4 cm
2 cm
6 cm

Example

Find the surface area of this solid.
Give your answer in cm².

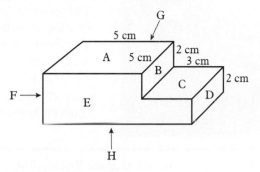

1 Label each face of the shape so that you do not miss any out.

2 Next, find the area of each face.

3 Add up all the areas to find the total surface area.
Area A: 5 cm × 5 cm = 25 cm²
Area B: 5 cm × 2 cm = 10 cm²
Area C: 5 cm × 3 cm = 15 cm²
Area D: 5 cm × 2 cm = 10 cm²
Area E: 5 cm × 4 cm + 3 cm × 2 cm = 26 cm²
Area F: 5 cm × 4 cm = 20 cm²
Area G: same as area E = 26 cm²
Area H: 8 cm × 5 cm = 40 cm²

Total surface area = 172 cm²

Exercise 7:2

Find the total surface area of these shapes.

1

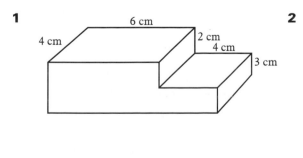

2

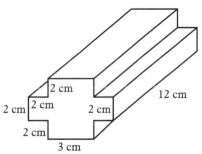

2 Volume and solids

This picture shows concrete being poured into the foundations of a new building. The engineer works out how much concrete she needs to fill the foundations. This means working out the volume of concrete she needs. The volume of concrete is measured in cubic metres.

| **Volume** | The amount of space that an object takes up is called its **volume**. |

Volume is measured in cubic units.
These can be **mm³, cm³** or **m³**.

| **1 cm³** | **1 cm³** is the space taken up by a cube with all its edges 1 cm long. |

| **Capacity** | The **capacity** of a hollow object is the volume of space inside it. |

| **1 m***l* | This cube has been filled with water. The volume of liquid inside is **1 millilitre**. This is written **1 m***l*. |

| **1 litre** | Larger volumes are measured in **litres**. 1 litre = 1000 m*l* |

A capacity of **1 m*l*** is the same as a volume of **1 cm³**.
1000 m*l* is the same as **1 litre**. 1 litre is written **1 *l***.

Exercise 7:3

1 a Look at this cuboid.
Imagine placing a layer of 1 cm cubes inside it to cover the base.
How many cubes could you fit on the base of the cuboid?

b How many layers of cubes could you fit inside the cuboid?

c How many cubes could you fit inside the cuboid altogether?
This is the volume of the cuboid.

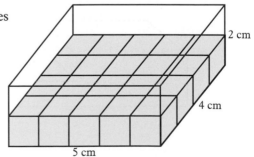

| **Volume of a cuboid** | To find the **volume of a cuboid** you need to work out how many 1 cm cubes will fit inside it. |

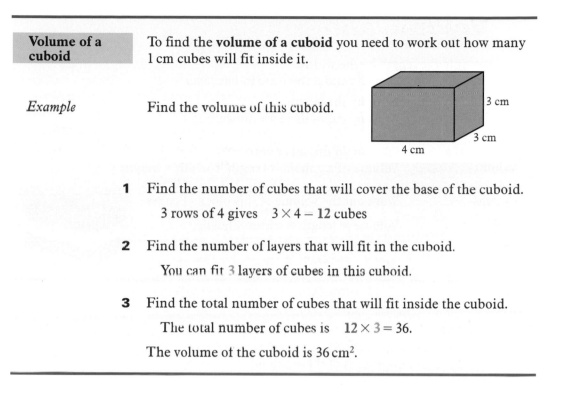

Example

Find the volume of this cuboid.

3 cm
3 cm
4 cm

1 Find the number of cubes that will cover the base of the cuboid.

3 rows of 4 gives $3 \times 4 = 12$ cubes

2 Find the number of layers that will fit in the cuboid.

You can fit 3 layers of cubes in this cuboid.

3 Find the total number of cubes that will fit inside the cuboid.

The total number of cubes is $12 \times 3 = 36$.

The volume of the cuboid is 36 cm^2.

---

2 Find the volume of each of these cuboids.

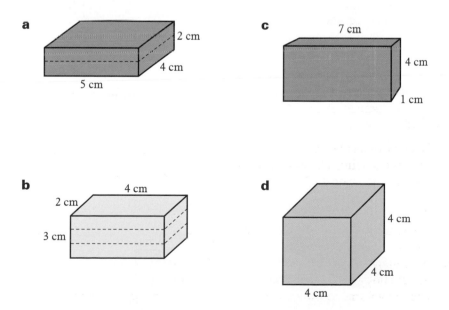

a

2 cm
4 cm
5 cm

c

7 cm
4 cm
1 cm

b

2 cm
4 cm
3 cm

d

4 cm
4 cm
4 cm

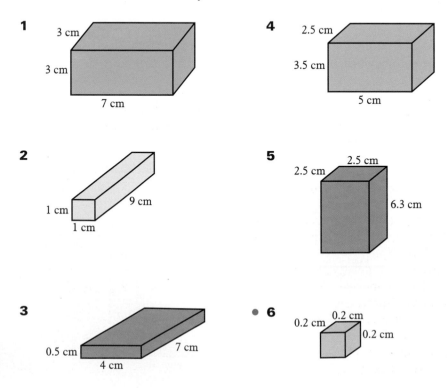

There is a faster way to find the volume of a block of cubes.

1 Multiply the length by the width.
   This tells you how many cubes there are in one layer.

2 Multiply your answer by the height.
   This tells you how many cubes there are altogether.

Volume of a cuboid	You can do this all at once: **Volume of a cuboid = length × width × height**

Example   Work out the volume of this block of cubes.

$$\text{Volume} = \text{length} \times \text{width} \times \text{height}$$
$$= 6 \times 3 \times 4$$
$$= 72 \text{ cm}^3$$

Exercise 7:4

Find the volume of each of these cuboids.
Use the rule above. Write your answers in cm³.

1 3 cm 3 cm 7 cm

4 2.5 cm 3.5 cm 5 cm

2 1 cm 1 cm 9 cm

5 2.5 cm 2.5 cm 6.3 cm

3 0.5 cm 4 cm 7 cm

● **6** 0.2 cm 0.2 cm 0.2 cm

Exercise 7:5

1 Andrew measures the dimensions of
this cereal box.
It is 7 cm by 19 cm by 29 cm.
Find the volume of the cereal box.

2 Katy measures the dimensions of
this orange juice carton.
It measures 5.9 cm by 9 cm by 19.5 cm.
Find the capacity of the carton.
Write your answer in m*l*.

3 Whirlwind tea bags come in two different
sizes of box.
The smaller box measures 8 cm by 8 cm
by 10 cm.
a Find the volume of the smaller box.
The larger box has twice the dimensions of
the smaller box.
b Find the volume of the larger box.

● **4** Standard bars of Universe chocolate measure 8 cm by 6 cm by 0.5 cm.
a How many **m*l*** of chocolate are in a standard bar of Universe?
The makers of Universe want to do a special offer of 50% extra free.
b What could they do to the dimensions of the bar?

● **5** Howard is digging a rectangular pond
in his garden.
He measures out the length and width of the
pond on the ground. It measures 2.5 m by
1.5 m. Howard digs to a depth of 0.5 m.
a Find the volume of earth that Howard has
to remove. Give your answer in **m³**.
b Work out how many cm³ there are in 1 m³.
(The answer is **not** 100.)
c Work out the volume of the pond in cm³.
d How many litres of water will Howard
need to fill the pond?

Composite shape	A **composite shape** is one that is made up of 2 or more simple shapes.

To find the volume of a composite shape:

1   Split the composite shape up into simple shapes.

2   Find the volume of each simple shape.

3   Add the volumes together to find the total volume.

Example   Find the volume of this solid.

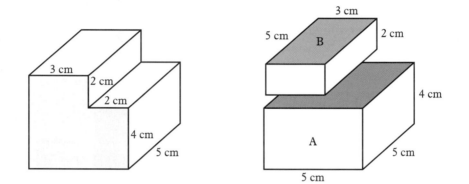

1   Split the shape up into two cuboids.
Label them A and B.

2   Volume of A = 5 cm × 5 cm × 4 cm = 100 cm³
Volume of B = 5 cm × 3 cm × 2 cm = 30 cm³

3   The total volume is 100 + 30 = 130 cm³

Exercise 7:6

Find the volume of each of these composite shapes.

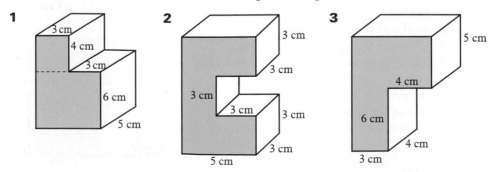

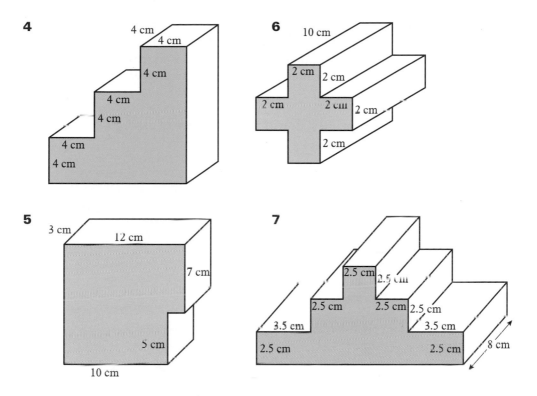

4

4 cm
4 cm
4 cm
4 cm
4 cm
4 cm
4 cm

6

10 cm
2 cm
2 cm
2 cm
2 cm
2 cm
2 cm

5

3 cm
12 cm
7 cm
5 cm
10 cm

7

2.5 cm
2.5 cm
2.5 cm
2.5 cm
2.5 cm
3.5 cm
3.5 cm
2.5 cm
2.5 cm
8 cm

These shapes have holes in them.
To find the volume of the shape:

a Find the volume of the shape as if the hole was not there.
b Find the volume of the hole.
c Subtract your answer to **b** from your answer to **a**.

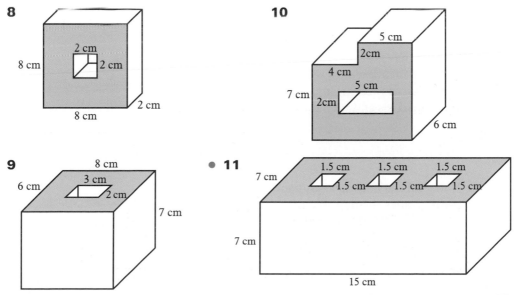

8

2 cm
8 cm
2 cm
2 cm
8 cm

10

5 cm
2cm
4 cm
7 cm
5 cm
2cm
6 cm

9

8 cm
3 cm
6 cm
2 cm
7 cm

11

7 cm
1.5 cm
1.5 cm
1.5 cm
1.5 cm
1.5 cm
1.5 cm
7 cm
15 cm

Limping seagulls

Limping seagulls are shapes that you make from a square piece of paper. Once you have a number of seagulls, you can fit them together to make different solids.

To make a limping seagull, start with a square piece of paper.

Fold the piece of paper in half and make a crease.

Open the paper up again and fold both edges into the middle.

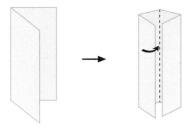

Fold the bottom right-hand corner up to the top.

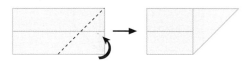

Turn the paper through 180° and do the same again.

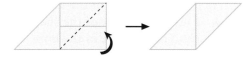

Open the paper up and you will find you have created two small triangles inside.
Fold both of these triangles back on themselves and tuck them under.

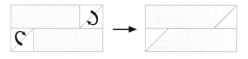

Now fold the bottom right hand corner under the flap above it where you have just folded the triangle.
Turn the paper through 180° and repeat.

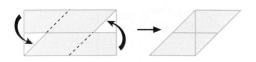

Next fold the two triangular pieces back on themselves so that they fold against the smooth side of the square centre piece.

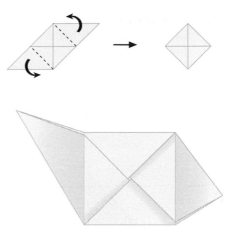

You now have a finished limping seagull!

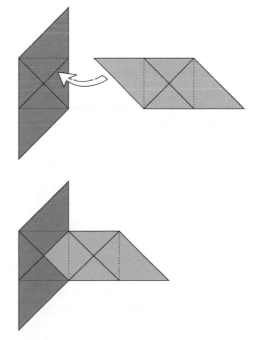

The triangular flaps enable limping seagulls to be fitted together to make models of various solids.
The easiest model to make is a cube.
You will need 6 limping seagulls to make a cube.

Once you have made 6 seagulls you need to learn how to fit them together.

There are two basic rules:
(1) Always hold the seagulls with the smooth side down.
(2) Seagulls always fit together at right angles to each other.

To fit two together:

Hold the first seagull vertically in your left hand and the second horizontally in your right hand.

Slide the two together so that the triangle of the horizontal seagull goes under the flap on the vertical one.

Hold the two seagulls that are linked in your left hand and hold another seagull horizontally in your right hand.

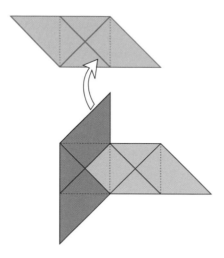

Slide the horizontal (green) seagull down onto the triangle at the top of the first (red) seagull.

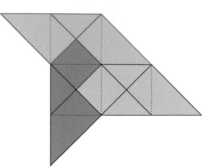

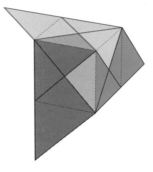

Fold the three seagulls so that the squares are now all at right angles to each other.
Link the new horizontal (green) seagull to the second (blue) one and you should now have three sides of your cube.

Continue adding the three remaining seagulls, linking the flaps as you go.
You should end up with a cube which is quite sturdy.

You can make other shapes with limping seagulls.
Experiment!
They look particularly effective made out of coloured paper.

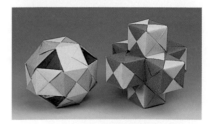

8 Probability

1 **Probability paper**

2 **Arrangements**

Eight is a cubic number

Eight times any triangular number is one less than a square number

There are eight notes in an octave

It is possible to place a maximum of eight queens on a chessboard so that none of them threatens any other

1 Probability paper

Rose and Edward are playing Snakes and Ladders.
Each of them has to get a six to start the game.
Edward says that this is unfair. He says that the 6 is the biggest score so it is the hardest to get.
He tells Rose that he wants to get a 1 to start.
Rose smiles happily and says OK!
Do you understand why she is happy?

Trial	In a probability experiment a **trial** is doing the experiment once. For throwing a dice, a trial is one roll of the dice.
Outcome	An **outcome** of a probability experiment is what you get by doing a trial. For throwing a dice, the outcomes are 1, 2, 3, 4, 5 and 6.
Success	In a probability experiment a **success** is when you get the outcome you want.
Relative frequency	When you do a probability experiment, **relative frequency** is an estimate of the probability. $$\text{Relative frequency} = \frac{\text{number of successes}}{\text{number of trials}}$$ If you roll a dice 100 times and you get a 6 twelve times then the relative frequency of getting a 6 is $\frac{12}{100} = 0.12$

Exercise 8:1

1 Emma throws a dice 100 times.
She gets a 6 fifteen times.
   a What is the relative frequency of getting a 6?
   b What is the relative frequency of not getting a 6?

2 Richard drops a piece of toast 50 times.
It lands butter side down 23 times.
   a What is the relative frequency of the toast landing butter side down?
   b What is the relative frequency of the toast landing butter side up?

3 Thomas throws a coin twice.
He gets a Head both times.
  a What is the relative frequency of Head?
Thomas thinks that the coin is biased.
  b Do you think that the coin is biased? Explain your answer.

4 James has a spinner with 5 equal sections.
They are coloured either red or blue.
After spinning the spinner 500 times,
the relative frequency of red is 0.18
  a How many red sections do you think there are on the spinner?
  b Do you know that your answer to **a** is definitely correct?
    Explain your answer.

As you repeat a probability experiment more and more times, the relative frequency tends towards the actual probability.
You can show this on a relative frequency diagram.

Lizzy is throwing a dice.
She is recording each throw and the number of 6s she has got so far.
She gets her first 6 on her third throw.
She works out the relative frequency after each throw by working out the number of 6s divided by the number of throws. She gives her values to 2 dp.

Throws	Number of 6s so far	Relative frequency (2 dp)
1	0	0.00
2	0	0.00
3	1	0.33
4	1	0.25
5	1	0.20
6	1	0.17
7	1	0.14
8	1	0.13
9	2	0.22
10	2	0.20

Now she plots the relative frequency against the number of throws like this.

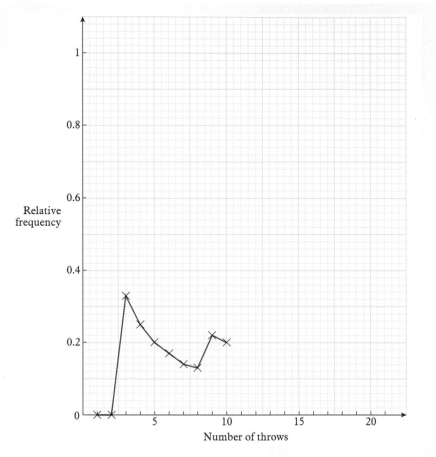

Of course, this is only 10 throws so the relative frequency graph hasn't settled down yet.
When the graph settles down, the value that it reaches gives you an estimate of the probability.

Exercise 8:2

1 Do Lizzy's experiment for yourself.
Use the same scale as Lizzy on the relative frequency axis.
Make sure that your horizontal axis has enough space for 100 throws.
You do not have to draw a table with all the results.
Just tally the number of throws and the number of 6s like this

Number of throws	Number of 6s
ЖН	I

and work out the relative frequency after each throw on your calculator.
Then you can plot the values as you go along.

2 Sue is throwing two coins.
She is recording the relative frequency of 2 Heads.
These are the outcomes for the first 50 throws.
Sue recorded her results going across each row in turn.

HT	HT	HH	TT	HT	HT	HT	HT	HH	HH
TT	HT	HT	HT	HH	TT	TT	HH	HT	HT
HH	HT	HH	TT	HT	HT	HT	HH	HT	HH
TT	TT	HH	HT	HT	TT	TT	HT	HT	HT
HT	HH	HT	HT	HT	HT	HH	HT	HH	HT

a Work out the relative frequency of 2 Heads after each of the 50 throws.

b Draw a relative frequency graph to show this information.

c Use your graph to estimate the probability of getting 2 Heads.

You need two dice in the next two questions.

3 Matt would like to know the probability of getting two 6s when he rolls two dice.
Do an experiment with two dice.
You will need to do enough trials to get a reasonably accurate result.
Draw a relative frequency graph and estimate this probability.
Tally the number of times you roll the two dice and the number of times you get two 6s like this:

Number of throws	Number times you get two 6s
ⱵⱵ ⱵⱵ ǀ	ǀǀ

Work out the relative frequency after each throw on your calculator.
Then you can plot the values as you go along.

4 Estimate the probability of scoring any double when you throw two dice.
You will need to do an experiment.
Do enough trials to get a reasonably accurate result.
Draw a relative frequency graph.
Use the graph to estimate the probability.

You don't always have to draw a relative frequency graph. You can use probability paper to record the results of experiments.

Probability paper looks like this.

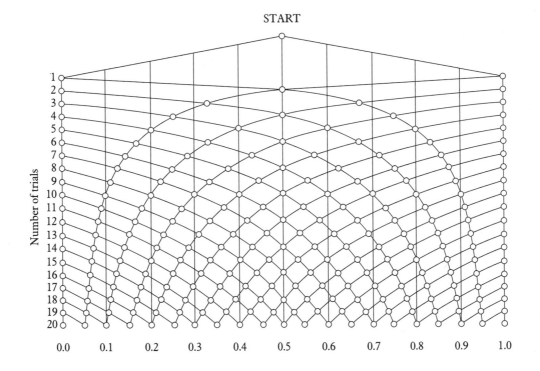

The number of trials goes down the page.

You start at the top of the page in the middle.

When you have a successful outcome you move to the right.

When you have a failure you move to the left.

You join the trail up as you go along.

The relative frequency is the value you reach at the bottom when you've done enough trials.

Exercise 8:3

1 The diagram shows the results of throwing a dice 20 times.
Success is throwing an even number.

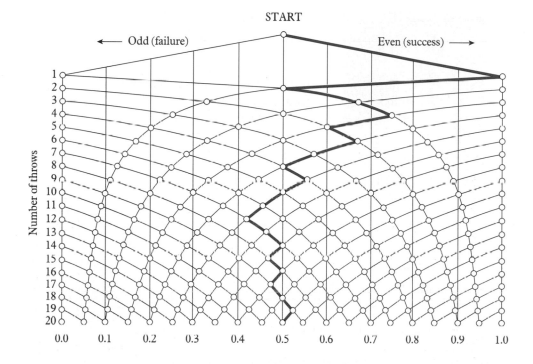

a What was the first outcome in the experiment?
b How many even numbers were there in the first 10 throws?
c Estimate the probability of getting an even number on a dice.

W 2 You need Worksheet 8:1 for this question.
Use the probability paper to record 20 results of each of these experiments.
a Throwing a coin. Success is getting a Tail.
b Throwing a dice. Success is getting a 1.

W 3 You need Worksheets 8:2 and 8:3 for this question.
Use the probability paper to record 100 results of each of these experiments.
a Throwing two coins. Success is getting a Head and a Tail.
b Throwing two dice. Success is getting double 4.

2 Arrangements

You have probably heard that the chance of winning the lottery is about 1 in 14 million.
This is because there are about 14 million ways of picking 6 numbers from the numbers 1 to 49.
This compares with a chance of 1 in 10 million of being killed in a plane crash. This is more likely than winning the jackpot!

Exercise 8:4

Rachael is designing flags. She has to decide how many stripes to have in each flag. She also needs to decide which colours to use to colour them in. She always uses a different colour for each of the stripes.

1 She starts with two stripes and uses two colours: red and blue.
  a Draw the flags that Rachael can make.
  b How many flags can she make?

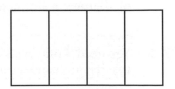

2 Now she has three stripes.
  She uses three colours: red, blue and green.
  a Draw the flags that Rachael can make.
  b How many flags can she make?

3 Now she has four stripes.
  She uses four colours: red, blue, green and yellow.
  a Draw the flags that Rachael can make.
  b How many flags can she make?

● **4** Look at your answers to questions **1–3**.
  How many flags can Rachael make with 5 stripes and 5 colours?
  Do not try to draw them all!

Exercise 8:5

1 Fran is making badges for sale at a summer fair.
She has pens in 3 colours: red, blue and green.
She has rectangular badges with 3 sections.
She uses a different colour for each of the sections.

This one is coloured red–blue–green.
How many different badges can she make?

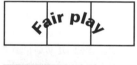

2 Richard sees that Fran's badges are selling well and decides to sell badges of his
own. He decides to use more colours.
He keeps the same basic design but uses 4 colours:
red, blue, green and yellow.
These badges have red as the first colour.

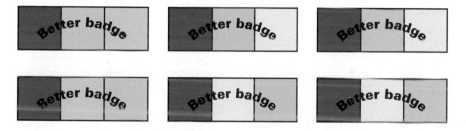

a Draw the badges that Richard can make with blue as the first colour.
b Draw the badges that Richard can make with green as the first colour.
c Draw the badges that Richard can make with yellow as the first
colour.
d How many different badges can he make?

3 Sam and Jane decide that they can top Richard's success by using even
more colours. They keep the same basic design but use 5 colours: red,
blue, green, yellow and purple. Here are a few of their badges.

How many badges can they make?
Do not try to draw them.
Think logically and follow the method in question **2**.

These are the results from Exercise 8:4

The number of ways of colouring 2 spaces with 2 colours is $2 = 2 \times 1$
The number of ways of colouring 3 spaces with 3 colours is $6 = 3 \times 2 \times 1$
The number of ways of colouring 4 spaces with 4 colours is $24 = 4 \times 3 \times 2 \times 1$
The number of ways of colouring 5 spaces with 5 colours is $120 = 5 \times 4 \times 3 \times 2 \times 1$

There is a quick way of writing this type of calculation.
If you want to multiply all the whole numbers starting with a whole number x and going down to 1 it is called x factorial. This is written $x!$ You will have this function on your calculator.

Look for your $x!$ key. It may be an $n!$ key on your calculator.

6 factorial is written 6!

This means $6 \times 5 \times 4 \times 3 \times 2 \times 1 = 720$

Key in $\boxed{6}$ $\boxed{x!}$ $\boxed{=}$

Exercise 8:6

1 How many ways are there to colour 7 spaces using 7 colours if no colour is used more than once?

2 Laura has a stall at the fair.
She has a rack with 8 slots and coloured balls in 8 colours.
She puts a coloured ball in each of the slots in the rack.
Each ball is a different colour.
People try to match the exact order of colours and if they succeed they win a car.
a How many ways are there to put the balls into the slots?
b What is the probability of winning the car? Give your answer as a fraction.

3 Work out

a $5! \times 3!$

b $\dfrac{10!}{4!}$

c $\dfrac{12!}{5!}$

d $\dfrac{10!}{6! \times 4!}$

e $\dfrac{14!}{8! \times 6!}$

f $\dfrac{20!}{12! \times 8!}$

4 The number of ways of choosing six numbers in the lottery is $\dfrac{49!}{43! \times 6!}$

a Work out the number of ways of choosing the winning numbers.
b Write down the probability of winning the lottery if you have one ticket. Give your answer as a fraction.

9 Algebra

1 **Collecting terms**

2 **Formulas**

Nine is a square number and is the sum of two triangular numbers

$9 = 1! + 2! + 3!$

Nine is written as 100 in base 3

Nine is the only square number that is the sum of two cubic numbers

The first nine integers can be placed in a magic square

1 Collecting terms

Ken is replacing the fence of the tennis court at Stanthorne High. The fence goes all around the outside of the court.

| **Perimeter** | The **perimeter** of a shape is the distance all round the outside. |

Example   Find the perimeter of each of these shapes.

a

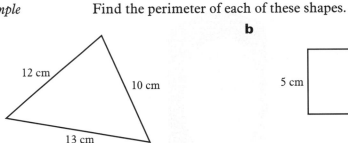

b

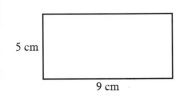

a Perimeter = 12 + 13 + 10 = 35 cm
b Remember to add the sides that aren't labelled.
   Perimeter = 5 + 9 + 5 + 9 = 28 cm

Exercise 9:1

1 Find the perimeter of each of these shapes.

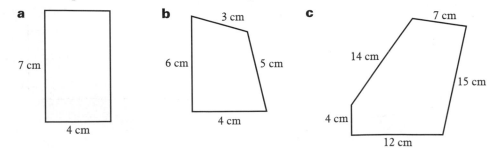

Example   Find the perimeter of each of these shapes.

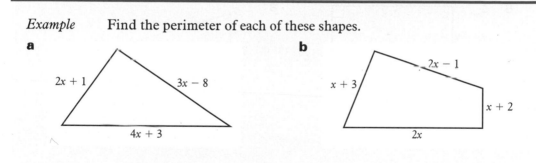

a   You add the lengths of the three sides together then collect like terms.
Perimeter $= 2x + 1 + 3x - 8 + 4x + 3$
$= 9x - 4$

b   Perimeter $= x + 3 + 2x - 1 + x + 2 + 2x$
$= 6x + 4$

Find the perimeter of each of these shapes.

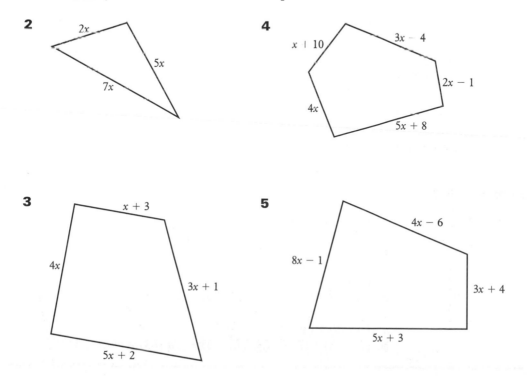

6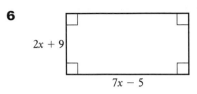

8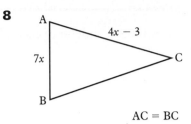

AC = BC

7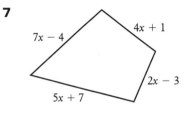

9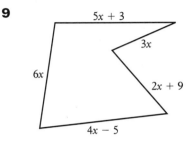

10 Work out the perimeter of:
  a an equilateral triangle of side d
  b a regular hexagon of side y
  c a regular octagon of side $3x$
  d a square of side $5y + 3$
  e a regular heptagon of side $4t - 3$
  f a regular decagon of side $2x + 7$
  g a regular dodecagon of side $9d - 6$
  h a regular nonagon of side $2x + y$

You can collect like terms $\quad\quad x \;+\; x \;+\; x \;=\; 3x$
You can also collect brackets $\quad (x + 2) + (x + 2) + (x + 2) = 3(x + 2)$

Example Collect these sets of brackets.
  a $(y + 5) + (y + 5)$
  b $(7a - 3) + (7a - 3) + (7a - 3) + (7a - 3)$

  a $(y + 5) + (y + 5) = 2(y + 5)$
  b $(7a - 3) + (7a - 3) + (7a - 3) + (7a - 3) = 4(7a - 3)$

Exercise 9:2

Collect these sets of brackets.

1 $(2b + 5) + (2b + 5) + (2b + 5)$

2 $(5t - 1) + (5t - 1) + (5t - 1) + (5t - 1) + (5t - 1) + (5t - 1)$

3 $(8y + 3) + (8y + 3) + (8y + 3) + (8y + 3)$

4 $(t + 7) + (t + 7) + (t + 7) + (t + 7) + (t + 7)$

5 $(2x - 3y) + (2x - 3y) + (2x - 3y) + (2x - 3y) + (2x - 3y) + (2x - 3y)$

6 $(4d + e) + (4d + e)$

Look at these two examples of collecting like terms:
$$a + 4 + a + 4 + a + 4 = 3a + 12$$
$$(a + 4) + (a + 4) + (a + 4) = 3(a + 4)$$

Both the left-hand sides are the same. So $3(a + 4)$ must equal $3a + 12$

To remove a bracket: multiply everything inside the bracket by the number outside.
$$3(a + 4) = 3 \times a + 3 \times 4 = 3a + 12$$

Example Multiply out these brackets:
    a $5(y - 3)$ **b** $2(7w + 3)$

    a $5(y - 3) = 5 \times y - 5 \times 3 = 5y - 15$
    b $2(7w + 3) = 2 \times 7w + 2 \times 3 = 14w + 6$

Multiply out these brackets.

7 $3(5r + 4)$ **12** $2(12c + 7)$

8 $2(2s - 6)$ **13** $5(8t - 1)$

9 $4(5t + 1)$ **14** $11(7a + 1)$

10 $6(5g + 4)$ **15** $12(7p + 9)$

11 $10(3h - 9)$ **16** $16(3d + 4)$

2 Formulas

Substitution is used a lot in sport. When a manager makes a substitution, one player on the pitch is replaced with another.
Substitution works the same way in maths.
When you substitute in maths you usually replace a letter with a number.

Example
$T = 3r^2 + 4$
Find the value of T when $r = 5$

You need to substitute the r with the 5
$r^2 = 5^2 = 5 \times 5$ so $T = 3 \times 25 + 4$
$\qquad = 25$ $\qquad\qquad\qquad = 79$

Sometimes you substitute for more than one letter.

Example
$V = u + at$
Find the value of V when $u = 3$, $a = 7$ and $t = 10$

You need to substitute for u, a and t.
u becomes 3, a becomes 7 and t becomes 10
$V = 3 + 7 \times 10$
$\quad = 3 + 70$
$\quad = 73$

Exercise 9:3

1 $D = 4s^2 - 3$ Find the value of D when s is:
    a 2   **b** 4   **c** 10

2 $A = 5t - v$ Find the value of A when:
  a $t = 6$ and $v = 9$
  b $t = 8$ and $v = 27$

3 $W = 5ab + 3c$ Find the value of W when:
  a $a = 4$, $b = 6$ and $c = 8$
  b $a = 5$, $b = 12$ and $c = 45$

4 $Q = h^3 - t^2$ Find the value of Q when:
  a $h = 5$ and $t = 7$
  b $h = 8$ and $t = 12$

5 $R = 2s^2 + a^2 - 6f$ Find the value of R when:
  a $s = 8$, $a = 3$ and $f = 11$
  b $s = 9$, $a = 20$ and $c = 25$

6 $B = 5d^3 - 3e^2$ Find the value of B when:
  a $d = 4$ and $e = 10$
  b $d = 6$ and $e = 8$

Number sequence	A **number sequence** is a pattern of numbers.

Term	Each number in the sequence is called a **term**. You can use the formula for a sequence to find the terms.

Example

The formula for a sequence is $T = 3n - 2$
Write down   **a**   the first four terms   **b**   the 30th term

a $n = 1$ for the 1st term so the 1st term $= 3 \times 1 - 2 = 1$
   $n = 2$ for the 2nd term so the 2nd term $= 3 \times 2 - 2 = 4$
   $n = 3$ for the 3rd term so the 3rd term $= 3 \times 3 - 2 = 7$
   $n = 4$ for the 4th term so the 4th term $= 3 \times 4 - 2 = 10$
b $n = 30$ for the 30th term so the 30th term $= 3 \times 30 - 2 = 88$

Exercise 9:4

1 The formula for a sequence is $T = 5n + 6$
Write down:
    a the first four terms   **b** the 30th term

2 The formula for a sequence is $T = 4n - 3$
Write down:
    a the first four terms   **b** the 30th term

3 The formula for a sequence is $T = 7n - 4$
Write down:
    a the first four terms   **b** the 50th term

4 The formula for a sequence is $T = 5n^2 + 6$
Write down:
    a the first four terms   **b** the 100th term

5 The formula for a sequence is $T = n^2 + 7n - 2$
Write down:
    a the first four terms   **b** the 10th term

6 Write down the first 5 terms of the sequence with the formula:
    a $T = 2n$ **d** $T = 10n$
    b $T = 3n$ **e** $T = 12n$
    c $T = 7n$ **f** $T = 20n$

7 Look at the pattern of your answers in question **6**.
What do you notice?

8 Write down the formula for each of these sequences.
    a 4, 8, 12, 16, 20, ...
    b 5, 10, 15, 20, 25, ...
    c 6, 12, 18, 24, 30, ...
    d 15, 30, 45, 60, 75, ...
    e 100, 200, 300, 400, 500, ...

9 Copy these. Join each sequence to the correct formula with an arrow.

$T = 5n + 3$	8, 17, 26, 35, 44, ...
$T = 3n + 5$	8, 11, 14, 17, 20, ...
$T = 9n - 1$	8, 13, 18, 23, 28, ...

Sometimes formulas for sequences have two parts.

Example   Find the formula for the sequence 3, 5, 7, 9, 11, ...

$$3 \quad 5 \quad 7 \quad 9 \quad 11$$
$$\quad +2 \quad +2 \quad +2 \quad +2$$

The rule to get to the next term is $+2$
The first part of the formula is $2n$

Write down the sequence for $2n$ 2, 4, 6, 8, 10, ...
Look to see what you have to do to the terms to get to the first sequence.
Here you have to $+1$ as $2 + 1 = 3$, $4 + 1 = 5$, $6 + 1 = 7$ and so on
The formula for the sequence is $T = 2n + 1$

Exercise 9:5

1 Find the formula for the sequence 7, 12, 17, 22, 27, ...
Copy this and fill in the missing numbers.

$$7 \quad 12 \quad 17 \quad 22 \quad 27$$
$$\quad +... \quad +... \quad +... \quad +...$$

The rule to get to the next term is ...
The first part of the formula is $...n$

Write down the sequence for $...n$ ..., ..., ..., ..., ..., ...
Look to see what you have to do to the terms to get to the first sequence.
Here you have to $+...$
The formula for the sequence is $T = ...n + ...$

2 Find the formula for the sequence 1, 5, 9, 13, 17, ...
Copy this and fill in the missing numbers.

1   5   9   13   17
+...   +...   +...   +...

The rule to get to the next term is ...
The first part of the formula is ...

Write down the sequence for ...   ..., ..., ..., ..., ..., ...
Look to see what you have to do to the terms to get to the first sequence.
Here you have to −...
The formula for the sequence is $T = ... − ...$

Find the formula for each sequence.

3 7, 10, 13, 16, 19, ...

4 4, 10, 16, 22, 28, ...

5 9, 11, 13, 15, 17, ...

6 9, 13, 17, 21, 25, ...

7 1, 6, 11, 16, 21, ...

8 12, 13, 14, 15, 16, ...

Example   The formula for a sequence is $T = 3n − 5$
Which term has the value 25?

$3 \times n − 5 = 25$ You have to find the value of n

$3 \times 10 − 5 = 25$ so $n = 10$

The **10**th term has the value 25.

---

9 The formula for a sequence is $T = 6n + 4$
Which term has the value 16?

10 The formula for a sequence is $T = 2n + 12$
Which term has the value 34?

11 The formula for a sequence is $T = 5n − 8$
Which term has the value 27?

10 Angles

1 **Constructions**

2 **Proof**

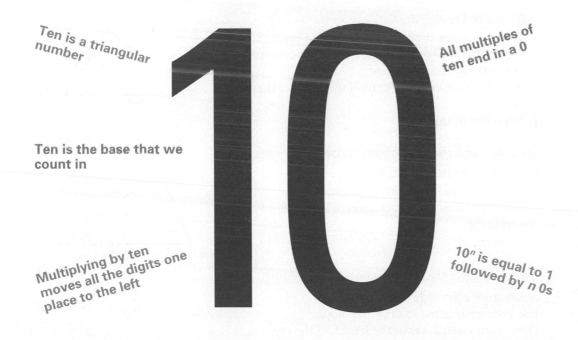

Ten is a triangular number

All multiples of ten end in a 0

Ten is the base that we count in

Multiplying by ten moves all the digits one place to the left

10^n is equal to 1 followed by n 0s

1 Constructions

An architect uses mathematical constructions to make sure that the drawings are accurate.

You need to be able to construct triangles.

These are the constructions that you need to know.
Always leave your construction lines on your diagrams to show that you have drawn them properly.

Three sides

Start by drawing the longest side as the base.
Use compasses to draw arcs for the other two sides.
Make sure that the arcs cross.
If they don't you need to extend them to get them to meet.
Join up the triangle.

One side and the two angles at the ends of the side

Draw the side that you're given as the base.
Use your protractor to draw the two angles.
Extend the sides until they meet. This gives you the triangle.

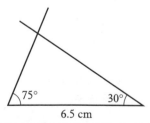

Two sides and the angle in between

Draw the longer side as the base.
Use your protractor to draw the angle.
Open your compasses to the length of the other side.
Make an arc to show this length.
Join up the missing side.

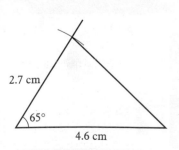

If you're not given a picture of the triangle it is always a good idea to draw a sketch first.

Exercise 10:1

1 For each part:
   (1) Construct the triangle.
   (2) Measure and write down the missing angles and lengths.

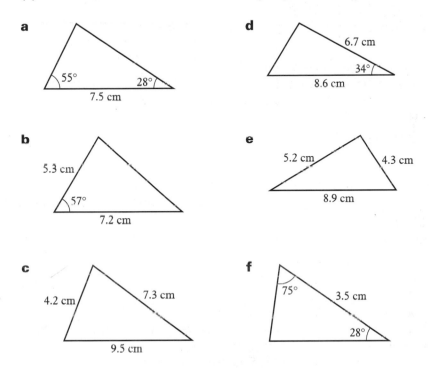

a

55° 28°
7.5 cm

d

6.7 cm
34°
8.6 cm

b

5.3 cm
57°
7.2 cm

e

5.2 cm 4.3 cm
8.9 cm

c

4.2 cm 7.3 cm
9.5 cm

f

75° 3.5 cm
28°

Questions **2–6** give you instructions about lengths and angles in triangles.

2 PQ = 4.2 cm, PR = 8.5 cm and QR = 7.1 cm
   a Draw a sketch of triangle PQR showing this information.
   b Construct triangle PQR.
   c Measure and write down the size of each of the angles of the triangle.

3 AB = 3.5 cm, ∠A = 35° and ∠B = 55°
   a Draw a sketch of triangle ABC showing this information.
   b Construct triangle ABC.
   c Measure and write down the length of side AC.

4 LM = 12.6 cm, LN = 14.2 cm and ∠L = 22°
    a Construct triangle LMN.
    b Measure and write down the length of side MN.

5 KL = 9.4 cm, ∠K = 45° and ∠L = 63°
    a Construct triangle JKL.
    b Measure and write down the length of side JK.

6 XY = 13.2 cm, YZ = 8.3 cm and ∠Y = 64°
    a Construct triangle XYZ.
    b Measure and write down the length of side XZ.

7 Look again at question **2**.
    a Draw a different triangle from the one you drew before.
       Start with a different side as the base.
    b Is your new triangle really different? Explain your answer.

8 Look again at questions **3–6**. For each question:
    a Try to draw a different triangle from the one you drew before.
       You must still follow the instructions given in the question.
    b Is your new triangle really different? Explain your answer.

Congruent

Shapes that are identical are called **congruent**.

The instructions you have been given for all of the constructions can only produce one triangle.

If you try to follow the instructions in a different order the triangle you get may look different but it will always be congruent to the first one that you draw.

If you compare the two triangles and the 3 sides of one triangle are equal to the 3 sides of the other triangle, then the two triangles are congruent.

You can remember this as SSS.

Triangles with 2 sides equal and the angle between the sides equal are congruent.

Remember this as SAS.

Triangles with 2 angles equal and the side between the 2 angles equal are congruent.

Remember this as ASA.

Exercise 10:2

1 For each pair of triangles:
(1) Decide if the triangles are congruent.
(2) If they are, write down the congruence rule that you have used.
Choose from SSS, SAS and ASA.

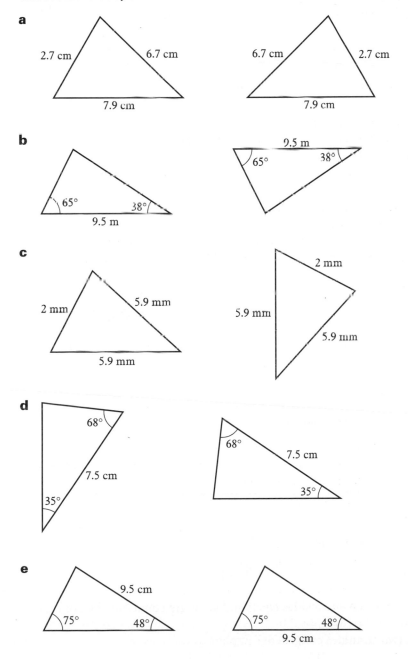

a

2.7 cm 6.7 cm 7.9 cm   6.7 cm 2.7 cm 7.9 cm

b

65° 38° 9.5 m   9.5 m 65° 38°

c

2 mm 5.9 mm 5.9 mm   2 mm 5.9 mm 5.9 mm

d

68° 7.5 cm 35°   68° 7.5 cm 35°

e

9.5 cm 75° 48°   75° 48° 9.5 cm

2 Here is a sketch of triangle ABC for you to construct.
Follow these instructions.

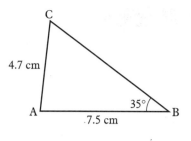

a Draw the 7.5 cm base.
b Draw the angle of 35° at B.
c Use your compasses to mark an arc for the point C.
d What goes wrong?

Not all sketches will give you a single solution.
When you try to construct the triangle in question **2** you find that the arc that you draw for point C cuts the side BC twice.
This means that you cannot construct the triangle.
You need more information to know which triangle is needed.

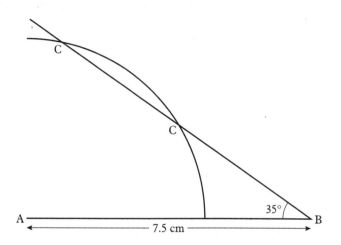

From the sketch above it looks as though the point that you need for C is the top one.

But you don't know for certain.

---

3 Construct triangle PQR so that PR = 11.4 cm, ∠R = 46° and PQ = 9.1 cm.
You should find that you get two triangles.

4 Two triangles have two sides equal and an angle equal but the angle is not between the two sides.
Are the two triangles congruent? Explain your answer.

2   Proof

Mathematicians are very interested in proof.

This is a picture of Professor Andrew Wiles. He proved Fermat's Last Theorem in 1995. Fermat had died without writing out his own proof of his theorem.

This theorem is easy to understand but it took the World's greatest mathematicians 358 years to finally prove it!

As an introduction to proof, in this section you are going to look at Geometrical proofs.
You have been told that the angles in a triangle add up to 180°.
How do you know that this is always true?
To prove this result you need to know some angle facts about parallel lines.

| **Parallel lines** | **Parallel lines** are always the same distance apart. |
| | You show parallel lines with arrows like this. |

When you draw a line across a pair of parallel lines you get these angles.

| **Alternate angles Z angles** | The red angles are called **alternate angles**. They are the angles in the Z shape. They are sometimes called **Z angles**. |

The blue angles are also alternate angles. They don't look much like a Z, but they are still alternate angles.

Alternate angles are equal.

| Corresponding angles F angles | The red angles are **corresponding angles**. They are the angles in the F shape so they are sometimes called **F angles**. | 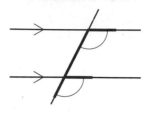 |

All the angles in the same place in the top part of the diagram and the bottom part of the diagram are corresponding angles.

Corresponding angles are equal.

Exercise 10:3

For each question, write down the angle marked with a letter. Give a reason for each answer.

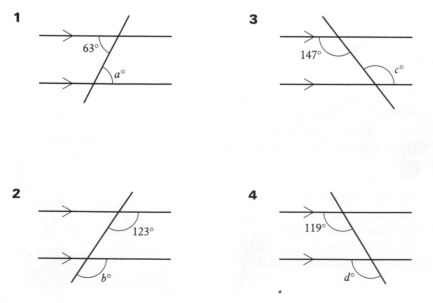

1   63°   a°

3   147°   c°

2   123°   b°

4   119°   d°

Now you're ready to prove that the angles in a triangle add up to 180°.
You already know that the angles on a straight line add up to 180°.
When you're writing out a proof you need to give a reason for every line
of your working.

This is triangle ABC.
The angles inside triangle ABC
are labelled a, b and c.
You need to show that $a + b + c = 180°$.

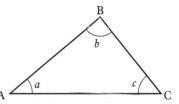

5　**a**　Sketch triangle ABC. Extend the line AC to the right and draw a line
parallel to AB from C to get this diagram. Label the angles p and q as
shown.

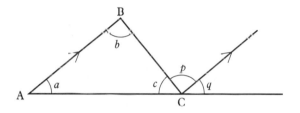

b　Copy this. Fill it in.

$$c + p + q = \dots \qquad \text{(Angles on ....)}$$
$$p = b \qquad \text{(.................. angles are equal)}$$
$$q = a \qquad \text{(.................. angles are equal)}$$

So　............ $= 180°$
and you have proved the result!

For the rest of the exercise you can use all the results that you know already.

These are the four results that you know:
　corresponding angles are equal
　alternate angles are equal
　the angles in a triangle add up to 180°
　isosceles triangles have two equal sides and the angles
　　at the ends of these sides are equal.

6 Prove that the angle outside triangle ABC at C is equal to the angles inside the triangle at A and B added together.

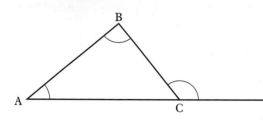

Hint: Use the proof that you used in question **5**.

7 ABC is an isosceles triangle.
CA = CB.
Prove that $s = 2t$

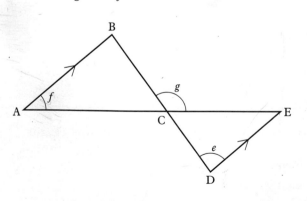

Hints: You need to work out the angle B in the triangle.
Then use the proof that you used in question **6**.

8 AB is parallel to DE.
Prove that $g = e + f$

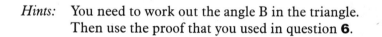

Hints: Find the angle at B in the triangle ABC.
You need to use the fact that AB is parallel to DE.
Now use the proof that you used in question **6**.
You can ignore the bottom part of the diagram now.

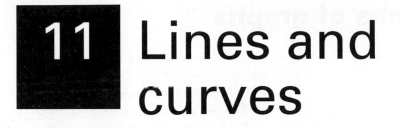

11 Lines and curves

1 Equations of graphs

2 Moving graphs

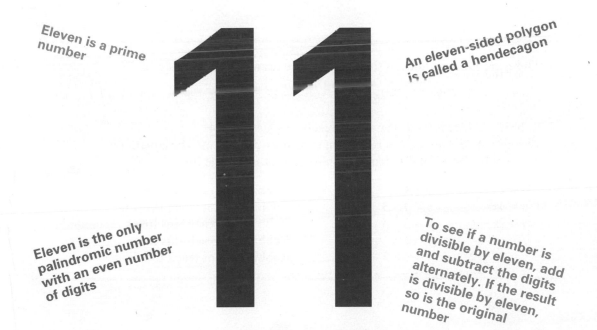

Eleven is a prime number

An eleven-sided polygon is called a hendecagon

Eleven is the only palindromic number with an even number of digits

To see if a number is divisible by eleven, add and subtract the digits alternately. If the result is divisible by eleven, so is the original number

1 Equations of graphs

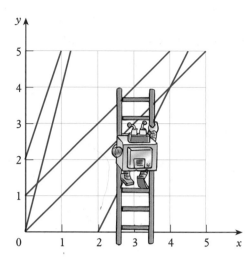

Robbie the robot is on a ladder.
The ladder is fixed to the grid.
Robbie can only reach some of the
lines drawn.
Which ones can he reach?

These are the equations of the lines that are drawn on Robbie's grid:

$$y = x \qquad y = 4x \qquad y = 2x - 4 \qquad y = x + 1 \qquad y = 3x + 2$$

Robbie's ladder is fixed at $x = 3$. It reaches as far as $y = 4$
To find which lines he can reach you substitute **3** for x into the equations.
If the value for y is more than 4, Robbie cannot reach the line.

$y = x$	$y = 3$	Robbie can reach this line.
$y = 4x$	$y = 4 \times 3 = 12$	Robbie cannot reach this line.
$y = 2x - 4$	$y = 2 \times 3 - 4 = 2$	Robbie can reach this line.
$y = x + 1$	$y = 3 + 1 = 4$	Robbie can reach this line.
$y = 3x + 2$	$y = 3 \times 3 + 2 = 11$	Robbie cannot reach this line.

Exercise 11:1

1 Robbie has a new ladder fixed at $x = 8$. This ladder can reach up to $y = 25$
Which of these lines can Robbie reach with his new ladder?
a $y = 3x - 5$ c $y = 4x - 12$ e $y = 5x + 1$
b $y = 3x + 2$ d $y = 7x - 10$ f $y = 6x - 4$

2 Mia has marked the point (4, 7) on a set of axes.
Mia is going to draw these lines on her axes.

$y = 3x$ $y = x + 5$ $y = 2x - 6$ $y = x - 8$

$y = x + 3$ $y = 2x - 1$ $y = 2x + 1$ $y = 10 - x$

a Which of these lines will pass under the point (4, 7)?

b Which will pass through the point (4, 7)?

Philip has drawn this line.
He has forgotten to label the line.
Which of these is the equation of the line?

$y = 3x - 1$

$y = x + 2$

$y = 2x + 1$

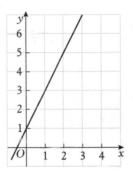

The line passes through the point (1, 3).

Substitute $x = 1$ into each of the equations.
The correct equation will give the answer 3.

$y = 3x - 1$	$y = 3 \times 1 - 1 = 2$	This is not the equation.
$y = x + 2$	$y = 1 + 2 = 3$	This could be the equation.
$y = 2x + 1$	$y = 2 \times 1 + 1 = 3$	This could be the equation.

You need to check another point.
This will tell you which of the two possible equations is correct.

The line passes through the point (2, 5).
Substitute $x = 2$ into each of the two remaining equations.

$y = x + 2$	$y = 2 + 2 = 4$	This is not the equation.
$y = 2x + 1$	$y = 2 \times 2 + 1 = 5$	This is the correct equation.

Always check two points on the line to see if you have the correct equation.

3 a Look at the line drawn on the grid. Write down the co-ordinates of two points that lie on the line.
b Which of these is the equation of the line?

$$y = x + 4$$
$$y = 3x - 2$$
$$y = 2x + 3$$

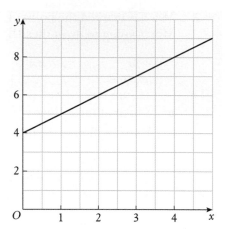

4 a Look at the line drawn on the grid. Write down the co-ordinates of two points that lie on the line.
b Which of these is the equation of the line?

$$y = x + 6$$
$$y = 3x + 4$$
$$y = 2x + 4$$

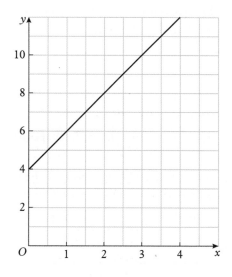

5 A line passes through the points (0, 5) and (10, 35). Which of these is the equation of the line?

$$y = 5x \qquad y = 3x + 5 \qquad y = 5x - 10$$

6 A line passes through the points (4, 3) and (7, 9). Which of these is the equation of the line?

$$y = x - 1 \qquad y = 3x - 12 \qquad y = 2x - 5$$

James is going to draw the graph of $y = 2x$

He draws a table of values.
The y values are all $2 \times$ the x values.

x	0	1	2	3
y	0	2	4	6

He plots the points $(0, 0)$, $(1, 2)$, and so on.
James joins the points with a straight line.
He extends his line to fill the axes.

James labels the line with its equation.

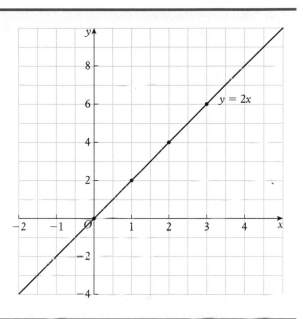

7 a Copy the axes.

b Copy and complete this table for the line $y = 2x + 3$

x	0	1	2	3
y	3			

c Plot the points from your table.
Draw the line $y = 2x + 3$
Label your line.

d Copy and complete this table for the line $y = 4x - 1$

x	0	1	2	3
y				11

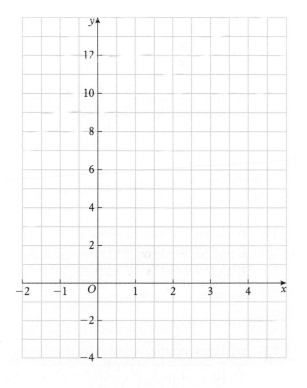

e Plot the points from your table.
Draw the line $y = 4x - 1$
Label your line.

f Write down the co-ordinates of the point of intersection of the two lines.

8 **a** Copy the axes.

b Copy and complete this table for the line $y = x + 4$

x	0	1	2	3
y		5		

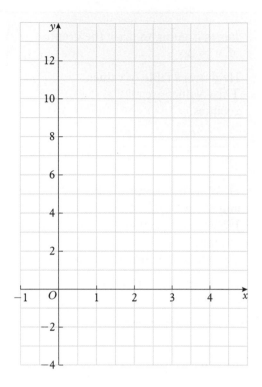

c Plot the points from your table.
Draw the line $y = x + 4$
Label your line.

d Copy and complete this table for the line $y = 3x + 2$

x	0	1	2	3
y				

e Plot the points from your table.
Draw the line $y = 3x + 2$
Label your line.

f Write down the co-ordinates of the point of intersection of the two lines.

9 **a** Draw another set of axes like those in question **8**.
b Draw and label the line $y = 3x - 4$
c Draw and label the line $y = 2x - 2$
d Write down the co-ordinates of the point of intersection of the two lines.

10 **a** Draw another set of axes like those in question **8**.
b Draw and label the line $y = 2x + 1$
c Draw and label the line $y = 2x + 3$
d What do you notice about the two lines?

11 **a** Draw another set of axes like those in question **8**.
b Draw and label the line $y = 3x - 2$
c Draw and label the line $y = 3x$
d What do you notice about the two lines?

12 **a** Copy these axes.
   b Draw and label the line $y = x$
   c Draw the line $y = x + 2$ on the same axes. Label the line.
   d Draw and label each of these lines on the same set of axes.

$y = x + 3$ $y = x + 6$
$y = x + 5$ $y = x - 1$

   e Write down what you notice about the lines that you have drawn.
   f For each line write down its equation and where it crosses the y axis. What do you notice?

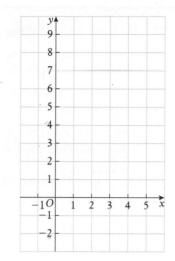

13 **a** Copy these axes.
   b Draw and label the line $y = 2x$
   c Draw the line $y = 2x + 1$ on the same axes. Label the line.
   d Draw and label each of these lines on the same set of axes.

$y = 2x + 3$ $y = 2x - 3$
$y = 2x - 1$ $y = 2x + \frac{1}{2}$

   e Write down what you notice about the lines that you have drawn.
   f For each line write down its equation and where it crosses the y axis. What do you notice?

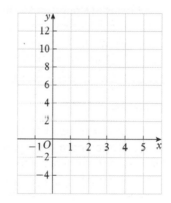

14 **a** Copy these axes.
   b Draw and label the line $y = x$
   c Draw the line $y = 2x$ on the same axes. Label the line.
   d Draw and label each of these lines on the same set of axes.

$y = 3x$ $y = 4x$ $y = \frac{1}{2}x$

   e Write down what you notice about the lines that you have drawn.

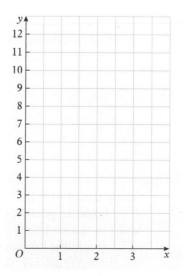

Two lines are parallel if the number multiplying the x is the same in both equations.

$y = 5x - 7$ and $y = 5x + 2$ are parallel
$y = 4x - 3$ and $y = 3x + 4$ are not parallel

The **number** on its own tells you where the line crosses the y axis.

$y = 5x + 2$ crosses the y axis at 2
$y = 4x - 3$ crosses the y axis at -3

Paula has drawn two straight lines.
She has labelled one line.
It is $y = 2x + 1$
She forgot to label the other.
What is its equation?

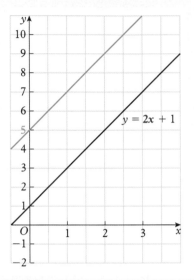

The lines are parallel so the equations start in the same way $y = 2x ...$
The green line crosses the y axis at 5 so the equation is $y = 2x + 5$

Exercise 11:2

In questions **1** to **8** the green and black lines are parallel.
Write down the equation of the green line in each question.

1

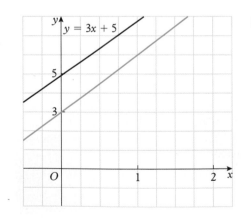

Copy this. Fill it in.
The lines are parallel so the equations start in the same way $y = ... x$
The green line crosses the y axis at ...
So the equation is $y = ... x + ...$

2

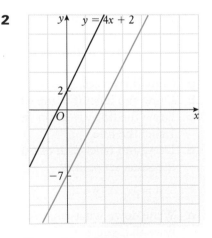

Copy this. Fill it in.
The lines are parallel so the equations start in the same way $y = ... x$
The green line crosses the y axis at $- ...$
So the equation is $y = ... x - ...$

3

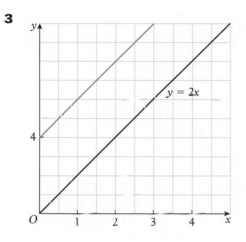

6

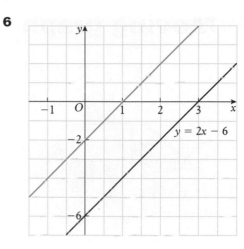

4

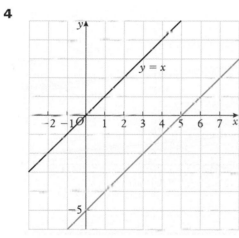

7

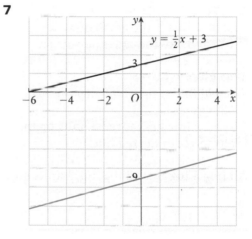

5

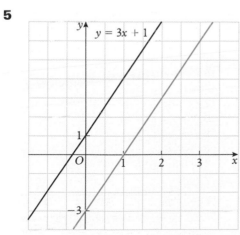

8

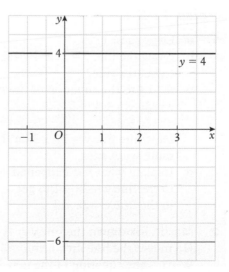

2 Moving graphs

Graphs can be moved by slightly changing their equation.

The blue line is the graph of $y = x + 2$
If you add 3 to the equation you get
   $y = x + 2 + 3$
This gives $y = x + 5$
The red line is the graph of $y = x + 5$

The blue line has moved 3 units up the y axis to get to the red line.

Adding 3 has moved the line 3 units up.

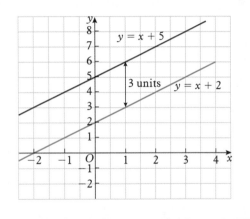

Exercise 11:3

1 a Copy these axes.
   b Draw the line $y = 2x - 1$
      Label the line.
   c Add 4 to the equation of the line.
      $y = 2x - 1 + 4$
      $y = 2x + 3$
      Draw the line $y = 2x + 3$ on the same set of axes.
   d Explain what has happened to the line $y = 2x - 1$ to get to the line $y = 2x + 3$

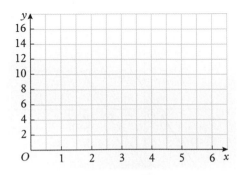

2 Martin has drawn the line $y = 4x + 3$
   He moves the line up 5 units.
   What is the equation of the new line?

3 Emma has drawn the line $y = 7x + 6$
She moves the line down 2 units.
What is the equation of the new line?

4 Write down the new equation when the line $y = 3x + 4$ is moved:
  a 4 units up
  b 3 units down
  c 7 units down
  d 4 units down

5 The graph of $y = 2x + 5$ has been moved. Write down the movement if
the new equation is:
  a $y = 2x + 8$
  b $y = 2x + 1$
  c $y = 2x$
  d $y = 2x - 3$

6 Write down the new equation when the line $y = 8x - 7$ is moved:
  a 4 units up
  b 3 units down
  c 9 units up
  d 7 units up

7 The graph of $y = 4x - 3$ has been moved. Write down the movement if
the new equation is:
  a $y = 4x - 1$
  b $y = 4x + 6$
  c $y = 4x$
  d $y = 4x - 7$

Some graphs are curves.
You need more points to draw a curve.
This is the table for $y = x^2$

x	-3	-2	-1	0	1	2	3
y	9	4	1	0	1	4	9

Each y number is the x number squared.
When the points are plotted they
do not lie in a straight line.

They are joined up with a curve.
The curve is labelled $y = x^2$

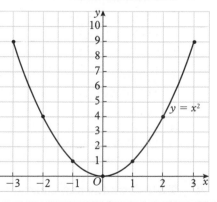

Exercise 11:4

1 Nina has added 3 to the equation $y = x^2$
The new equation is $y = x^2 + 3$
  a Copy the table for $y = x^2 + 3$
    Fill it in.

x	-3	-2	-1	0	1	2	3
y	12						

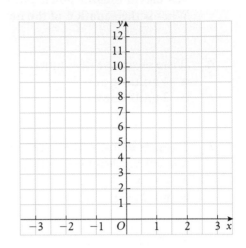

  b Copy the axes and draw the
    curve $y = x^2 + 3$
  c You have added 3 to the
    equation $y = x^2$
    How far up has the graph of
    $y = x^2$ moved?

2 Leroy has subtracted 2 from the
equation $y = x^2$
The new equation is $y = x^2 - 2$
  a Copy the table for $y = x^2 - 2$
    Fill it in.

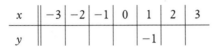

x	-3	-2	-1	0	1	2	3
y					-1		

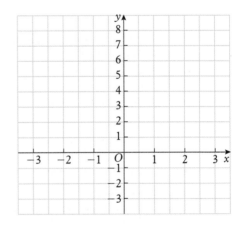

  b Copy the axes and draw the
    curve $y = x^2 - 2$
  c You have subtracted 2 from the
    equation $y = x^2$
    How has the graph of
    $y = x^2$ moved?

3 **a** Emma has drawn the curve $y = x^2 + 6$
    She moves the curve down 4 units.
    What is the equation of the new curve?
  b Luke has drawn the curve $y = x^2 - 3$
    He moves the curve up 7 units.
    What is the equation of the new curve?

4 Write down the new equation when the curve $y = x^2$ is moved:
  a 4 units up   **c** 7 units down
  b 3 units down   **d** 10 units up

5 The graph of $y = x^2$ has been moved. Write down the movement if the new equation is:

a $y = x^2 + 9$ **c** $y = x^2 - 7$
b $y = x^2 - 5$ **d** $y = x^2 + 12$

6 Write down the new equation when the curve $y = x^2 + 7$ is moved:

a 2 units up   **c** 7 units down
b 5 units down   **d** 9 units down

7 The graph of $y = x^2 - 5$ has been moved.
Write down the movement if the new equation is:

a $y = x^2 - 1$ **c** $y = x^2 + 2$
b $y = x^2 - 7$ **d** $y = x^2$

8 You are going to draw the curve $y = x^3$

a Copy the table for $y = x^3$
Fill it in.

x	-4	-3	-2	-1	0	1	2	3	4
y	-64	-27					8		

b Copy the axes.
c Plot the points from the table.
Join them with a curve.
Label the curve.
d Add 3 to the curve equation to get $y = x^3 + 3$
e Draw a new table for $y = x^3 + 3$
f On the same set of axes draw the curve of $y = x^3 + 3$
Label your curve.
g How has the curve $y = x^3$ moved to get to the curve $y = x^3 + 3$?

9 Sheila has drawn the curve $y = x^3$
She moves the curve down 4 units.
What is the equation of the new curve?

10 Write down the new equation when the curve $y = x^3$ is moved:
   a 8 units up   **c** 9 units down
   b 6 units down   **d** 1 unit up

11 The graph of $y = x^3$ has been moved. Write down the movement if the new equation is:
   a $y = x^3 + 10$ **c** $y = x^3 - 6$
   b $y = x^3 - 3$ **d** $y = x^3 + 4$

12 Write down the new equation when the curve $y = x^3 + 4$ is moved:
   a 3 units up   **c** 1 unit down
   b 4 units down   **d** 12 units down

13 The graph of $y = x^3 - 4$ has been moved.
Write down the movement if the new equation is:
   a $y = x^3 - 2$ **c** $y = x^3 + 5$
   b $y = x^3 - 6$ **d** $y = x^3$

14 This is the curve $y = x^2 + x$

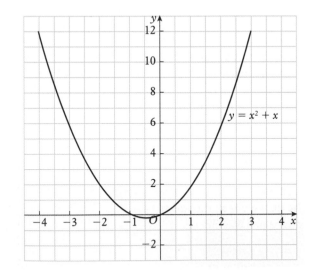

Write down the new equation when the curve is moved:
   a 3 units down
   b 5 units up

● **15** The graph of $y = x^2 + x + 4$ has been moved.
Write down the movement if the new equation is:
   a $y = x^2 + x + 9$ **c** $y = x^2 + x - 3$
   b $y = x^2 + x + 1$ **d** $y = x^2 + x - 15$

12 Units and networks

1 Weird units

2 Networks

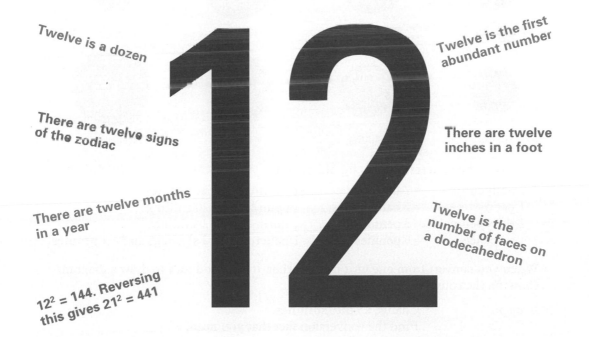

Twelve is a dozen

Twelve is the first abundant number

There are twelve signs of the zodiac

There are twelve inches in a foot

There are twelve months in a year

Twelve is the number of faces on a dodecahedron

$12^2 = 144$. Reversing this gives $21^2 = 441$

1 Weird units

This is a picture of money used in the UK until 1971 when we adopted the decimal system.
Before then you had to know how to convert units of money. This was not as simple as it is now that there are 100 pence in a pound!

These are some of the coins used in the old money system.

Farthing	Halfpenny	Penny	Threepenny bit

Sixpence	Shilling	Florin	Haifcrown

These are the conversion facts for old money.

1 halfpenny	= 2 farthings	1 shilling	= 12 pennies
1 penny	= 2 halfpennies	1 pound	= 20 shillings
1 threepenny bit	= 3 pennies	1 florin	= 2 shillings
1 sixpence	= 6 pennies	1 halfcrown	= 2 shillings and six pennies

When you convert from one unit into another, it is a good idea to draw a diagram showing the conversion number.

Example

Change £3 into shillings.
Find the conversion fact that you need.
1 pound = 20 shillings
20 is the conversion number.
Now draw a diagram for changing pounds into shillings

pounds ——— × 20 ——→ shillings

So   £3 = 3 × 20 = 60 shillings

Exercise 12:1

1 a Copy this diagram.
   Fill in the missing number.

   florins ——— × ... ——→ shillings

b Change each of these into shillings.
   (1) 2 florins　　　(2) 5 florins　　　(3) 12 florins

2 a Copy this diagram.
   Fill in the missing number.

   shillings ——— × ... ——→ pennies

b Change each of these into pennies.
   (1) 3 shillings　　　(2) 8 shillings　　　(3) 12 shillings

3 a Copy this diagram.
   Fill in the missing number.

   pennies ——— × ... ——→ farthings

b Change 1 penny to farthings.
c Change each of these into farthings.
   (1) 4 pennies　　　(2) 7 pennies　　　(3) 14 pennies

Example　　Convert 80 shillings into pounds.

Here is the diagram for changing pounds into shillings

　　pounds ——— × 20 ——→ shillings

If you want to change shillings into pounds you can reverse the diagram.
The opposite of multiplying is dividing so the reverse diagram is

　　pounds ←——— ÷ 20 ——— shillings

So divide by 20 to change shillings into pounds.

So 80 shillings = 80 ÷ 20 = 4 pounds

---

4 a Copy this diagram.
   Fill in the missing number.

   pennies ←——— ÷ ... ——— farthings

b Change each of these into pennies.
   (1) 4 farthings　　　(2) 20 farthings　　　(3) 48 farthings

5 **a** Copy this diagram.
Fill in the missing number.

florins ⟵——— ÷ ... ——— shillings

b Change each of these into florins.
(1) 2 shillings   (2) 18 shillings   (3) 46 shillings

6 **a** Copy this diagram.
Fill in the missing number.

threepenny bits ⟵——— ÷ ... ——— pennies

b Change each of these into threepennybits.
(1) 6 pennies   (2) 36 pennies   (3) 60 pennies

7 **a** Write down the conversion fact
for the halfcrown from p. 132.
b How many pennies are there in a shilling?
c What fraction of a shilling is 6 pennies?
d Copy this diagram.
Fill in the missing number.

halfcrowns ——— × ... ⟶ shillings

e Change each of these into shillings.
(1) 2 halfcrowns   (2) 6 halfcrowns   (3) 5 halfcrowns
f Draw the reverse diagram for converting shillings to halfcrowns.
g Change each of these into halfcrowns.
(1) 10 shillings   (2) 7.5 shillings   (3) 17.5 shillings

Example   Convert 3 shillings into farthings.

This needs two stages.

1 shilling = 12 pennies and 1 penny = 4 farthings

This is the diagram to change shillings into farthings

shillings ——— × 12 ⟶ pennies ——— × 4 ⟶ farthings

So   3 shillings = 3 × 12 × 4 farthings
= 144 farthings

Exercise 12:2

1 **a** Copy this diagram.
Fill in the missing numbers.

pounds ——— × ... ——→ shillings ——— × ... ——→ pennies

b Change 1 pound to pennies.
c Change each of these into pennies.
(1) 2 pounds   (2) 5 pounds   (3) 10 pounds

2 **a** Copy this diagram.
Fill in the missing numbers.

florins ——— × ... —— ▸ shillings ——— × ... ——→ pennies

b Change 1 florin to pennies.
c Change each of these into pennies.
(1) 3 florins   (2) 4 florins   (3) 11 florins

3 **a** Copy this reverse diagram for changing pennies into pounds.
Fill in the missing numbers.

pounds ◂ —— ÷ ... ——— shillings ◂——— ÷ ... ——— pennies

b Change each of these into pounds.
(1) 240 pennies   (2) 720 pennies   (3) 1200 pennies

4 **a** Draw a diagram for changing sixpences into farthings.
b Change 1 sixpence into farthings.
c Draw a diagram for changing farthings into sixpences.
d Change each of these into sixpences.
(1) 48 farthings   (2) 72 farthings   (3) 144 farthings

5 **a** Copy this diagram.
Fill in the missing numbers.

halfcrowns ——— × ... ——→ shillings ——— × ... ——→ pennies

b Change each of these into pennies.
(1) 2 halfcrowns   (2) 4 halfcrowns   (3) 5 halfcrowns
c Draw the reverse diagram for changing pennies into halfcrowns.
d Change each of these into halfcrowns.
(1) 90 pennies   (2) 180 pennies   (3) 600 pennies

6 About 50 years ago the coins used in India were pies, annas and rupees.

  1 anna = 12 pies
  1 rupee = 16 annas

a Copy this diagram to show how to change annas into pies.

  annas ——— × ... ——→ pies

b Draw a diagram to show how to change:
(1) rupees to annas   (2) rupees to pies

c Change each of these.
(1) 1 anna into pies   (4) 3 annas into pies
(2) 7 rupees into annas   (5) 1 rupee into pies
(3) 4 rupees into pies   (6) 4 rupees into annas

d Copy this reverse diagram to show how to change pies into annas.

  annas ←——— ÷ ... ——— pies

e Draw the reverse diagram to show how to change:
(1) annas into rupees   (2) pies into rupees

f Convert each of these.
(1) 24 pies into annas   (4) 84 pies into annas
(2) 48 annas into rupees   (5) 1920 pies into rupees
(3) 576 pies into rupees   (6) 80 annas into rupees

7 The units of currency in a land far, far away are malcs, sags, pooks and stues.

  1 sag = 9 malcs
  1 pook = 10 sags
  1 stue = 3 pooks

a Draw diagrams to help you change:
(1) sags into malcs   (4) stues into malcs
(2) pooks into sags   (5) sags into stues
(3) stues into pooks   (6) malcs into stues

b Change each of these.
(1) 5 sags into malcs   (4) 2 stues into malcs
(2) 4 pooks into sags   (5) 360 sags into stues
(3) 3 stues into pooks   (6) 540 malcs into stues

2   Networks

This is a photo of the town of Kaliningrad, previously called Köningsberg.

There is a famous problem, called the Köningsberg Bridge Problem, which you are going to solve in this section.

First, you need to know a little about networks.

Network	A **network** is a diagram that has a number of points joined by lines. The points usually represent places or positions and the lines represent routes between them.
Node	A **node** is a point on the network where lines meet. The network above has 4 nodes.
Arc	An **arc** is a line joining two nodes on the network. The network above has 6 arcs.
Power of a node	The **power of a node** is the number of arcs that are coming out of it. The 3 blue arcs come out of the red node. The red node has a power of 3.
Route	A **route** is a path that can be drawn through the network with one continuous line. Each arc can only be used once. Starting from the red node the numbered arrows show you a route around this network. This route finishes at the blue node. This is not the only route around the network.

Exercise 12:3

1 For each of the networks:
   (1) Write down the number of nodes.
   (2) Write down the number of arcs.
   (3) Write down the power of the red node.
   (4) Copy the network and draw a route around it.

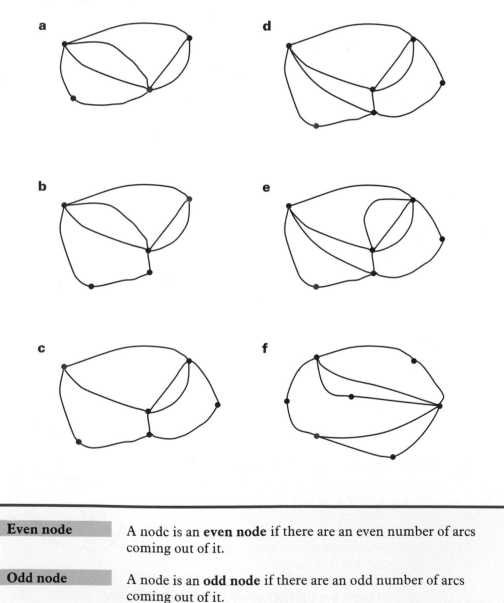

| **Even node** | A node is an **even node** if there are an even number of arcs coming out of it. |

| **Odd node** | A node is an **odd node** if there are an odd number of arcs coming out of it. |

2 For each of the networks:
   (1) Write down the power of each of the nodes.
   (2) Write down the number of even nodes.
   (3) Write down the number of odd nodes.
   (4) Copy the network and draw a route around it *if you can.*

You will need to start at each of the nodes in turn.
Once you find a route you can stop checking that network.

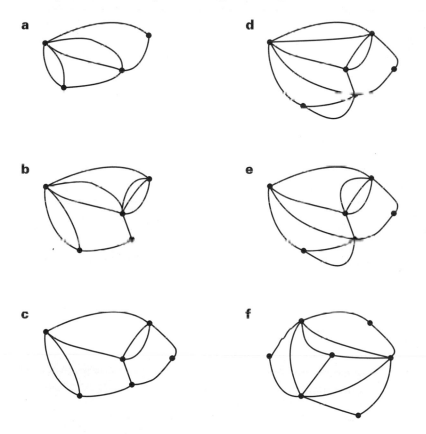

3 Look again at the networks in question **1**.
   It is possible to draw a route around all of them.
   Count the number of even and odd nodes for each of these networks.

4 Can you write down a rule that tells you if it is possible to draw a route
   around a network? Look at the number of odd nodes!

Euler was the first mathematician to spot that a route is only possible around a network if there are no odd nodes or exactly 2 odd nodes. He used this knowledge to solve the Köningsberg Bridge Problem. the town has a complicated bridge pattern across the river that flows around it.

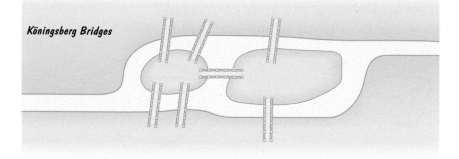

Köningsberg Bridges

The Köningsberg Bridge Problem is this:

Is it possible to walk around the town so that you can start and finish at the same point and only cross each bridge once?

5 This is a network that represents the town.
Each bridge is an arc and each separate piece of ground is a node.
Solve the Köningsberg Bridge Problem.

| **Region** | A **region** is a space bounded by one or more arcs. The outside of a network is a region. This network has four regions. |  |

---

6 Look again at all the networks in questions **1** and **2**.
   a Draw a table like this and fill it in. You will need 12 rows.

Network	Regions	Nodes	Arcs
1a			

   b Find a rule that connects regions, nodes and arcs for all networks.

13 Algebra: into the unknown

1 Brackets and equations

2 Changing the subject

The fear of the number thirteen is called triakaidekaphobia

Thirteen is a prime number

There are thirteen cards in each suit in a pack

1 Brackets and equations

The temperature one winter morning in Nottingham was −3°C. If you multiply this temperature by 11 you get the temperature of Trondheim in Norway on the same morning. Imagine how cold that is!

Directed numbers	**Directed numbers** are numbers with signs in front of them. For example $-4, +7, -2, -8$ are directed numbers.

Example

Use a calculator to answer these.
  a $-3 \times +4$ **b** -5×-2

a   Key in:

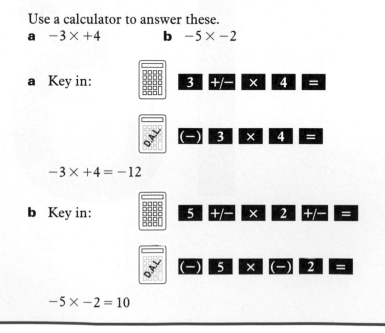

$-3 \times +4 = -12$

b   Key in:

$-5 \times -2 = 10$

Exercise 13:1

1 Work these out using your calculator.

a -9×5 **d** -2×-7 **g** 3×-8

b -7×-5 **e** 9×-4 **h** $(-8)^2$

c -1×-12 **f** 2×-11 **i** $(-6)^2$

2 Use your answers to question **1** to answer these.

a What happens when you multiply two negative numbers together?

b What happens when you multiply a negative number by a positive number?

When you multiply two negative numbers together, the answer is **positive**.

For example $-3 \times -8 = 24$

When you multiply a positive number by a negative number the answer is **negative**.

For example $-6 \times 7 = -42$

When you square a negative number, the answer is always **positive**.

For example $(-5)^2 = -5 \times -5 = 25$

This is because you are multiplying a negative number by a negative number.

When you cube a negative number, the answer is always **negative**.

For example $(-2)^3 = -2 \times -2 \times -2 = -8$

This is because squaring gives you a positive number. You then multiply this square by a negative number to get the cube.

---

3 Work these out. Do not use a calculator.

a -3×-5 **d** $(-4)^2$ **g** 6×-10

b -7×12 **e** $(-5)^3$ **h** -11×-9

c -13×3 **f** -20×-70 **i** $(-10)^3$

Example Simplify these: **a** $2a \times -4$ **b** $-7 \times -4x$

a $2a \times -4 = -8a$ since $2 \times a \times -4 = 2 \times -4 \times a$
$$= -8 \times a$$
$$= -8a$$

b $-7 \times -4x = 28x$ since $-7 \times -4 \times x = 28 \times x$
$$= 28x$$

---

4 Simplify these:

a $4 \times -3y$ **g** $8a \times 11$
b $-8 \times -2a$ **h** $-7 \times -g$
c $12 \times 5h$ **i** $8 \times -5w$
d $4y \times 8$ **j** $-9t \times -3$
e $-6 \times -4s$ **k** $-3y \times 12$
f $6t \times -7$ **l** $-9 \times -3w$

To remove a bracket you multiply everything inside the bracket by the number outside.

Example Multiply out these brackets:

a $3(4x - 6)$ **b** $-5(3y - 2)$ **c** $-2(4t + 6)$

a $3(4x - 6)$ $= 3 \times 4x$ $+ 3 \times -6$
$$= 12x - 18$$

b $-5(3y - 2) = -5 \times 3y$ -5×-2
$$= -15y + 10$$

c $-2(4t + 6) = -2 \times 4t$ $-2 \times +6$
$$= -8t - 12$$

---

5 Multiply out these brackets:

a $5(4s + 3)$ **g** $-4(9 + 7y)$
b $3(6 + 4x)$ **h** $-5(7 + w)$
c $-6(5x - 9)$ **i** $-8(8 - 2x)$
d $7(4 + 3s)$ **j** $5(2y - 9z)$
e $-2(6y - 8)$ **k** $-9(5a - 7b)$
f $7(12 - 7s)$ **l** $-4(1 - 5t)$

Once you have multiplied out a bracket you can look for like terms to collect.

Example

Expand the brackets and collect like terms.

a $7x - 3(x - 7)$

b $4(2x + 6) + 7x - 2(3x - 4)$

a $7x - 3(x - 7)$ means you need to multiply the $(x - 7)$ by -3

$-3(x - 7) = -3x + 21$ because $-3 \times x = -3x$

and $-3 \times -7 = 21$

So $7x - 3(x - 7) = 7x -3x + 21$

$= 4x + 21$

b $4(2x + 6) + 7x - 2(3x - 4) = 8x + 24 + 7x - 6x + 8$

$= 9x + 32$

6 Expand the brackets and collect like terms.

a $8 + 3(7f - 2)$

b $3(5x + 8) - 4x + 6$

c $7(3t + 8) - 4(2t - 5)$

d $7 - 3(6y - 5)$

e $8a + 2(6 - 3a) - 7$

f $3(2a + 3b) - 2(4a - 9b)$

7 Expand the brackets and collect like terms.

a $4(2y + 4) + 7(3y - 2) - 5(y - 6)$

b $7(4x - 8) - 3(2x + 1) + 6(x - 4)$

c $2(7 - 6k) + 3(2k + 5) - 8(k - 3)$

Equations sometimes have brackets.

If an equation has brackets you need to multiply out the brackets before you can solve it.
When you have multiplied out the brackets you collect like terms.
You then solve the equation as usual.

Example Solve $2(3x - 4) + 5 = 39$

$$2(3x - 4) + 5 = 39 \qquad \text{Multiply out the brackets}$$
$$6x - 8 + 5 = 39 \qquad \text{Collect like terms on the left}$$
$$6x - 3 = 39 \qquad \text{Add 3 to both sides}$$
$$6x = 42 \qquad \text{Divide both sides by 6}$$
$$x = 7$$

Exercise 13:2

Solve these equations.

1 $6(2x + 3) = 54$

2 $6(7x - 2) = 72$

3 $6 + 2(4y - 3) = 40$

4 $5(2a + 3) - 4(8 - a) = 11$

5 $4(2x - 6) + 3(x - 2) = 25$

6 $3(2a + 3) - 2(a + 4) = 45$

7 $26 - (t + 4) + 2(t - 3) = 28$

8 $7x - 4(x - 2) + 25 = 57$

9 $5(3x + 7) - 3(4x - 11) = 98$

10 $3(7x - 4) + 2(3x - 17) = 197$

Look at the equation $8a = 5a + 21$
It has letters on both sides.
To solve it, you start by changing the equation so that a is only on one side.

Example Solve $8a = 5a + 21$

Look to see which side has the least a.
In this example the right-hand side has only $5a$.
Subtract $5a$ from both sides to start. This gets the as on one side only.

$$8a = 5a + 21 \qquad \text{Subtract } 5a \text{ from both sides}$$
$$3a = 21 \qquad \text{Divide both sides by 3}$$
$$a = 7$$

Sometimes the left-hand side will have the least number of letters.

Example

Solve $\quad 3y + 28 = 7y$

The left-hand side has only $3y$ so you subtract $3y$ from both sides.

$$3y + 28 = 7y \qquad \text{Subtract } 3y \text{ from both sides}$$
$$28 = 4y \qquad \text{Divide both sides by 4}$$
$$7 = y$$
$$y = 7 \qquad \text{Write the equation the other way round so}$$
$$\text{that the letter is on the left}$$

Exercise 13:3

Solve these equations.

1 $\quad 7x = 5x + 14$

3 $\quad 4(3x + 6) = 18x$

2 $\quad 18 + 3y = 6y$

4 $\quad 14 - 3(2 - 3f) = 11f$

Example

Solve $\quad 2(5x - 1) - (x + 3) = 3(4x + 1) - 7x$

$$2(5x - 1) - (x + 3) = 3(4x + 1) - 7x \qquad \text{Multiply out the brackets}$$
$$10x - 2 - x - 3 = 12x + 3 - 7x \qquad \text{Collect like terms on both sides}$$
$$9x - 5 = 5x + 3 \qquad \text{Subtract } 5x \text{ from both sides get}$$
$$\text{the } xs \text{ on one side only}$$
$$4x - 5 = 3 \qquad \text{Add 5 to both sides}$$
$$4x = 8 \qquad \text{Divide both sides by 4}$$
$$x = 2$$

5 $5(2x - 9) = 23 + 2(x + 2)$

6 $2(3a + 4) - 5(6 - 2a) = 4(a - 5) + 34$

7 $9(2s + 1) + 1 = 5(6s - 4) - 3(8 - 2s)$

8 $7(4 - 2x) + 35x = 5(3x - 1) + 4(8x + 5)$

9 $9(2y - 1) + 2(3y - 4) + 2 = 12y + 6(5y - 4)$

10 $2(5m - 4) + 3(4 + 2m) - 5(m - 8) = 7(3m + 1) - 4(7 - 4m) + 13$

In questions **11** to **14** write down an equation that must be true for the diagram.
Then solve the equation.

11

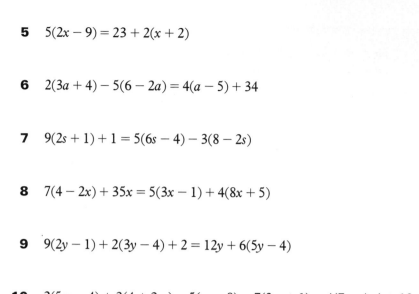

13

12

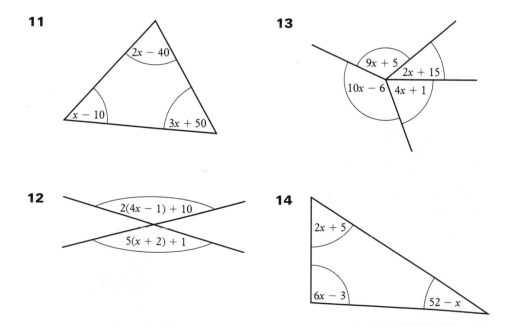

14

Some equations have fractions in them.

To solve the equation $8 = \dfrac{x}{3}$ you multiply both sides of the equation by 3.

This gets rid of the fraction.

$$8 = \frac{x}{3} \qquad \text{Multiply both sides by 3 to get rid of the fraction}$$
$$24 = x$$
$$x = 24$$

Now look at the equation $\quad 8 = \dfrac{32}{x}$

You treat the x as you did the 3 before.

$$8 = \frac{32}{x} \qquad \text{Multiply both sides by } x \text{ to get rid of the fraction}$$
$$8x = 32 \qquad \text{Divide both sides by 8}$$
$$x = 4$$

Exercise 13:4

Solve these equations.

1 $\quad 22 = \dfrac{x}{5}$

2 $\quad 5 = \dfrac{40}{x}$

3 $\quad 12 = \dfrac{48}{x}$

4 $\quad \dfrac{y}{5} = 6$

5 $\quad 2 = \dfrac{16}{x}$

6 $\quad 6 = \dfrac{42}{y}$

7 $\quad 15 = \dfrac{90}{a}$

8 $\quad \dfrac{20}{w} = 4$

You have seen trial and improvement as a way of solving more complicated equations.

Example

Solve this equation by trial and improvement

$$x^2 - 9x + 14 = 0$$

There are two answers between 0 and 10.

Value of x	Value of $x^2 - 9x + 14$	
1	$1^2 - 9 \times 1 + 14 = 6$	too big
2	$2^2 - 9 \times 2 + 14 = 0$	correct
3	$3^2 - 9 \times 3 + 14 = -4$	too small
6	$6^2 - 9 \times 6 + 14 = -4$	too small
7	$7^2 - 9 \times 7 + 14 = 0$	correct

The solutions are $x = 2$ and $x = 7$

You can draw a curve of the left-hand side of the equation.

Example

Complete the table of values for $y = x^2 - 9x + 14$
Use the table to draw the graph of $y = x^2 - 9x + 14$

x	0	2	4	6	8	10
x^2	0			36		
$-9x$	0	-18			-72	-90
14	14	14	14			
y	14					

The 1st row lists the values of x that you need to substitute.

The red row shows the values of x^2.

The blue row shows the values of $-9x$.
For example when $x = 4$, $-9x = -9 \times 4$
$$= -36$$

The 14s in the green row do not change.

The bottom row shows the values of y.
You add the values in each column to get the y values.

x	0	2	4	6	8	10
x^2	0	4	16	36	64	100
$-9x$	0	-18	-36	-54	-72	-90
14	14	14	14	14	14	14
y	14	0	-6	-4	6	24

To draw the curve you plot the points (0, 14), (2, 0) and so on.

Join the points with a curve.

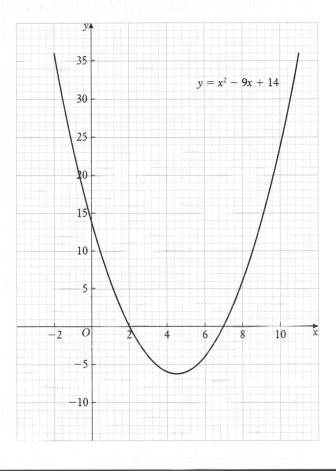

$y = x^2 - 9x + 14$

Exercise 13:5

1 **a** Solve this equation by trial and improvement $x^2 - 12x + 27 = 0$
There are two answers between 0 and 10.

b Copy this table of values. Fill it in.

x	0	2	4	6	8	10
x^2	0					
$-12x$	0	-24				
27	27					
y	27	-5				

c Copy the axes from the example.
Use the table of values to draw the graph of $y = x^2 - 12x + 27$

2 **a** Solve this equation by trial and improvement
$$x^2 - 13x + 40 = 0$$
There are two answers between 0 and 10.

b Copy this table of values. Fill it in.

x	0	2	4	6	8	10
x^2	0					
$-13x$	0					
40						
y						

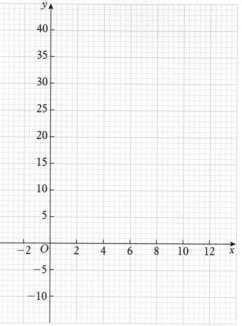

c Copy the axes.
Draw the graph of $y = x^2 - 13x + 40$

3 **a** Solve this equation by trial and improvement $x^2 - 7x + 6 = 0$
There are two answers between 0 and 10.

b Draw a table of values. Fill it in.

c Copy the axes from question **2**.
Draw the graph of $y = x^2 - 7x + 6$

4 **a** Solve this equation by trial and improvement $x^2 - 7x + 10 = 0$
There are two answers between 0 and 10.

b Draw a table of values. Fill it in.

c Copy the axes from question **2**.
Draw the graph of $y = x^2 - 7x + 10$

● **5** Look at your answers to part **a** and the curves you have drawn in part **c**
for each of questions **1** to **4**.
Can you see the connection between the solutions to the equation and
the curves you have drawn?
Can you explain the connection?

2 Changing the subject

Penny is always very good at changing the subject when her Dad asks her if she has done her homework.
She is not quite as good at changing the subject in algebra.

You use inverses to change the subject of a formula.
The inverse of 'square' is 'square root'.
The inverse of 'cube' is 'cube root'.

Example	Make y the subject of $\quad 3x = y^2 - 7$
$3x = y^2 - 7$	Write the equation the other way round
	The new subject is now on the left
$y^2 - 7 = 3x$	Add 7 to both sides
$y^2 = 3x + 7$	Now you square root both sides
$y = \sqrt{3x + 7}$	Make sure you show that all of the right-hand side is square rooted

Exercise 13:6

Change the subject of these formulas to the letter in red.

1 $\quad y = x^2 + 8$ $\qquad x$

2 $\quad s = 5t^2 - 3$ $\qquad t$

3 $\quad S = r^3 - 2$ $\qquad r$

4 $\quad L = \sqrt{m - 6}$ $\qquad m$

5 $\quad G = (x + 4)^2$ $\qquad x$

6 $\quad A = \sqrt{8b - c}$ $\qquad b$

7 $\quad V = (2g + 1)^3$ $\qquad g$

8 $\quad y = 3x^2 - 12$ $\qquad x$

9 $\quad h = 5t^3 + 4$ $\qquad t$

10 $\quad V = \dfrac{4}{3}\pi r^3$ $\qquad r$

Example Make d the subject of $4a = \sqrt[3]{7d + 6} - c$

$4a = \sqrt[3]{7d + 6} - c$ Write the equation the other way round

$\sqrt[3]{7d + 6} - c = 4a$ You need the cube root on its own, so add c to both sides

$\sqrt[3]{7d + 6} = 4a + c$ Cube both sides
Use brackets to show you are cubing the whole of the right-hand side

$7d + 6 = (4a + c)^3$ Subtract 6 from both sides

$7d = (4a + c)^3 - 6$ Divide both sides by 7

$d = \dfrac{(4a + c)^3 - 6}{7}$

● **Exercise 13:7**

Change the subject of these formulas to the letter in red.

1 $G = \sqrt{a - 5} + c$ *a*

2 $3x = \sqrt{4y - 2} + 5z$ *y*

3 $m = \sqrt[3]{8s - 5} + 10$ *s*

4 $y = (2x - 3)^2$ *x*

5 $d = (3e + 5)^3$ *e*

6 $c = (2a - 1)^2 + 4$ *a*

7 $f = (4h - 5)^3 - 8$ *h*

8 $r = \dfrac{\sqrt{6s - 5t}}{8}$ *s*

14 Compound areas

1 **Compound areas**

2 **Pick's theorem**

Fourteen is the third square pyramidal number

There are fourteen pounds in one stone

There are fourteen days in a fortnight

1 Compound areas

Rod runs a business that puts new wall coatings on buildings.

The cost depends on the area to be covered. Rod has to work out the area of the walls of this house. The areas of the doors and windows do not count when working out the cost.

Compound area   A **compound area** is an area that is built up of two or more simple shapes.

Some shapes have pieces cut out of them. To find the area of this type of shape you find the total area of the shape as if the cut out pieces weren't there. Then you find the area of the cut out pieces and subtract them from the original area.

Example   Find the area of this shape. Give your answer in cm².

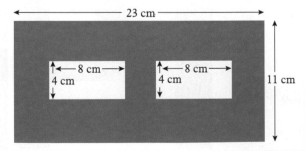

The area of the shape if the white pieces weren't cut out would be $23 \times 11 = 253 \, \text{cm}^2$

The area of one of the white pieces is $8 \times 4 = 32 \, \text{cm}^2$
There are two white pieces so the white area is $2 \times 32 = 64 \, \text{cm}^2$
The red area is $253 - 64 = 189 \, \text{cm}^2$

Exercise 14:1

Find the coloured area of each of these shapes.
Show clearly how you have worked out the area in each question.

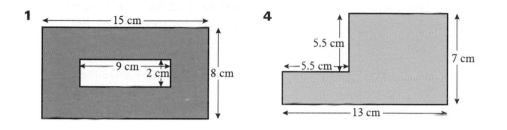

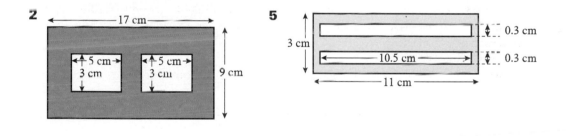

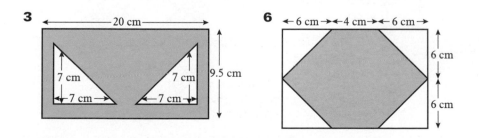

7

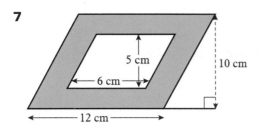

10

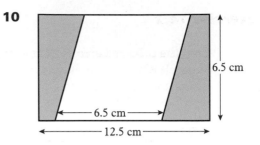

8

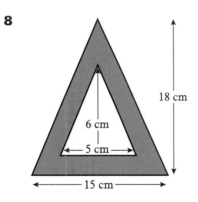

11

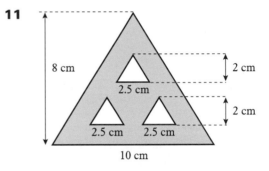

9

12

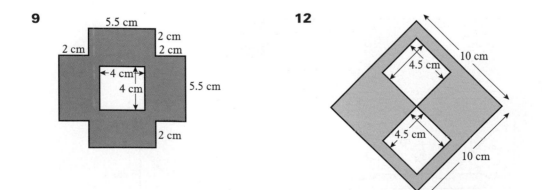

Exercise 14:2

This is a plan of the front of one of the houses that Rod is going to pebble dash.
There are three windows and a door that must not be counted when working out the area to be covered.

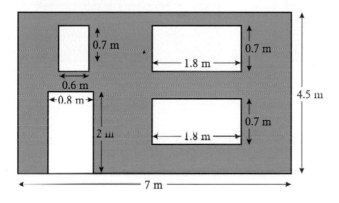

1   Work out the total area of the windows and doors.

2   Work out the area that needs to be pebble dashed.
Show your working clearly.

3   The cost of pebble dashing is £23.50 per square metre.
Work out the cost of pebble dashing this wall.
Give your answer to the nearest £.

These are the plans of the back and sides of the house.

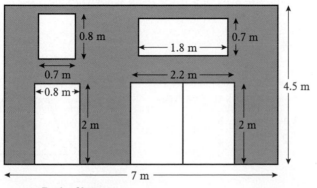

Back of house

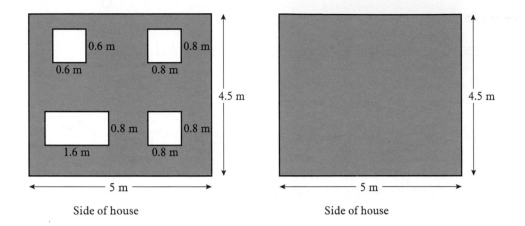

Side of house   Side of house

4 Work out the area of the back of the house that needs pebble dashing.

5 Work out the area of the two sides of the house that need pebble dashing.

6 Work out the cost of pebble dashing for the whole house, including the front.

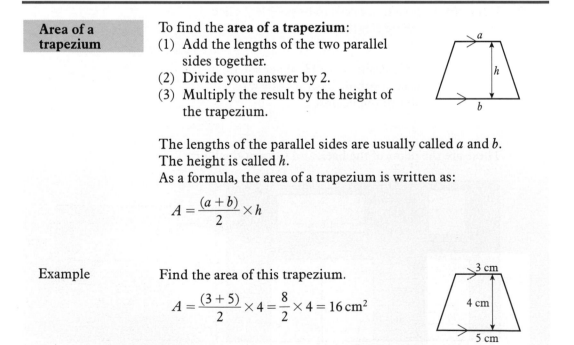

Area of a trapezium

To find the **area of a trapezium**:
(1) Add the lengths of the two parallel sides together.
(2) Divide your answer by 2.
(3) Multiply the result by the height of the trapezium.

The lengths of the parallel sides are usually called a and b.
The height is called h.
As a formula, the area of a trapezium is written as:

$$A = \frac{(a+b)}{2} \times h$$

Example

Find the area of this trapezium.

$$A = \frac{(3+5)}{2} \times 4 = \frac{8}{2} \times 4 = 16 \, \text{cm}^2$$

Exercise 14:3

Find the area of each of these trapeziums.

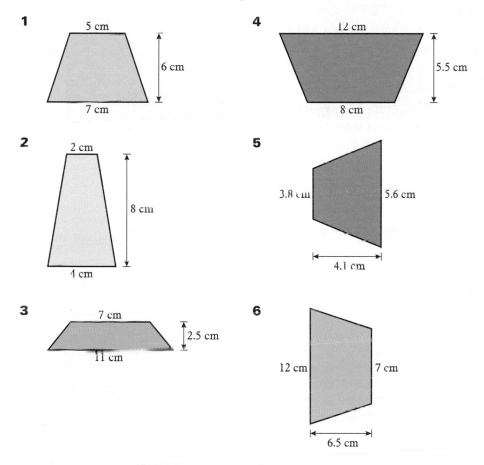

1   5 cm   6 cm   7 cm

2   2 cm   8 cm   4 cm

3   7 cm   2.5 cm   11 cm

4   12 cm   5.5 cm   8 cm

5   3.8 cm   5.6 cm   4.1 cm

6   12 cm   7 cm   6.5 cm

7   Find the area of each of these plastic stencils.

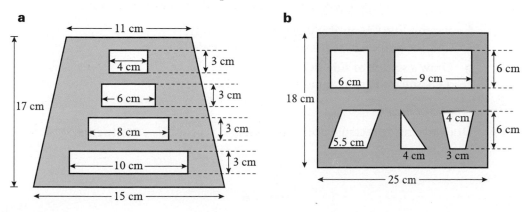

a   11 cm   3 cm   4 cm   3 cm   6 cm   3 cm   8 cm   3 cm   10 cm   17 cm   15 cm

b   6 cm   9 cm   6 cm   18 cm   5.5 cm   4 cm   4 cm   3 cm   6 cm   25 cm

Exercise 14:4 Constructions

1 This construction produces a triangle which has the same area as the quadrilateral you start with.

    a Copy the quadrilateral ABCD. It does not have to be exact.

    b Join B to D with a straight line.

    c Extend AD with a dotted line.

    d Draw a line from C parallel to BD. Mark the point where it crosses your dotted line E.

    e Join B to E.

Triangle ABE has the same area as ABCD.

2 Draw two more quadrilaterals of your own and repeat this construction.

3 This construction produces a square with the same area as the rectangle you start with.

    a Draw a rectangle and label it ABCD.

    b Extend AB with a dotted line.

    c Put your compass point on B and pencil point on C. Draw an arc from C to meet your dotted line. Mark this point E.

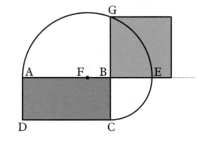

    d Find the midpoint of AE and mark it F.

    e Put your compass point on F and your pencil point on A. Draw a semicircle from A to E.

    f Extend line CB until it meets the semi-circle. Call the point where it meets the semi-circle G.

    g Draw a square of side BG. This square has the same area as ABCD.

4 Draw two more rectangles of your own and repeat this construction.

2 Pick's theorem

Ned sometimes wished he had a garden with a smaller perimeter!

Pick's theorem is a rule that links the perimeter and the area of some special types of shape.

It is worth noting that normally there is no link between area and perimeter.

Look at these two diagrams:

This shape has a large perimeter but quite a small area.

This shape has a much smaller perimeter but a bigger area.

Exercise 14:5

You will need 1 cm square dotty paper throughout this exercise.

1 **a** Copy this shape on to dotty paper.
b Write down the number of dots on the perimeter of the shape.
c Write down the area of the shape.

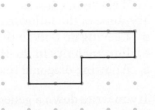

2 **a** Copy this shape.
   b Write down the number of dots on the perimeter of the shape.
   c Write down the area of the shape.

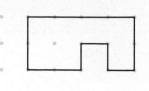

3 Draw 6 more shapes of this type. They must have vertical and horizontal sides only. They must also have exactly one dot in the middle.

4 **a** Copy this table. Allow 8 rows altogether.

Shape number	Dots on perimeter	Area	Dots inside
1			1
2			1
3			1

   b Enter the data from all 8 shapes into your table.
   c Look at the 'Dots on perimeter' and 'Area' columns of your table. Write down a link between the area and the perimeter of these shapes. Write your rule in algebra if you can.

5 **a** Draw 5 shapes which are similar to those in question **3** but have **two** dots in the middle.
   b Draw a table as you did for the previous set of shapes. Fill it in.
   c Write down the link between the area and the perimeter for this type of shape.

6 Repeat the process for shapes with three dots in the middle.

7 **a** Predict the rule linking area and perimeter for shapes with four dots in the middle.
   b Draw some shapes and test your prediction.

8 Write down predictions for the next few sets of shapes. Test each one by drawing some diagrams.

9 Try some of the following:
   a Leaving no dots in the centre of the shapes.
   b Putting holes in the shapes.
   c Allowing diagonal lines as sides.

10 Try to write down a general rule that works for all shapes. This is Pick's theorem.

15 Small parts

1 **Algebraic fractions**

2 **Recurring decimals**

Fifteen is the first product of two odd primes

There are fifteen red balls in a snooker triangle

Fifteen is the magic number for a magic square using the numbers 1 to 9

1 Algebraic fractions

The letters felt a fraction of their former selves!

Adding fractions

You already know that you can add fractions when the bottom numbers are the same.
This is still true if the fractions involve algebra.

Example   Simplify   **a** $\dfrac{x}{3} + \dfrac{x}{3}$ **b** $\dfrac{2x}{7} + \dfrac{3x}{7}$

a $\dfrac{x}{3} + \dfrac{x}{3} = \dfrac{2x}{3}$

b $\dfrac{2x}{7} + \dfrac{3x}{7} = \dfrac{5x}{7}$

When the two bottom numbers are different, you must make them the same.
This is called finding a common denominator.

Example   Simplify $\dfrac{2x}{3} + \dfrac{x}{6}$

$$\overset{\times 2}{\underset{\times 2}{\dfrac{2x}{3} = \dfrac{4x}{6}}}$$

So $\dfrac{2x}{3} + \dfrac{x}{6} = \dfrac{4x}{6} + \dfrac{x}{6} = \dfrac{5x}{6}$

Exercise 15:1

1 $\dfrac{x}{5}+\dfrac{x}{5}$

2 $\dfrac{2x}{7}+\dfrac{3x}{7}$

3 $\dfrac{5x}{13}+\dfrac{6x}{13}$

4 $\dfrac{x}{2}+\dfrac{x}{4}$

5 $\dfrac{x}{3}+\dfrac{x}{6}$

6 $\dfrac{2x}{5}+\dfrac{x}{10}$

7 $\dfrac{x}{6}+\dfrac{3x}{12}$

8 $\dfrac{5x}{7}+\dfrac{3x}{14}$

9 $\dfrac{6x}{11}+\dfrac{5x}{11}$

10 $\dfrac{4x}{3}+\dfrac{7x}{12}$

11 $\dfrac{x}{2}+\dfrac{x}{3}$

12 $\dfrac{x}{3}+\dfrac{x}{4}$

13 $\dfrac{2x}{3}+\dfrac{x}{5}$

14 $\dfrac{3x}{7}+\dfrac{2x}{3}$

15 $\dfrac{5x}{7}+\dfrac{x}{10}$

● **16** $\dfrac{3x}{7}+\dfrac{5x}{6}$

17 $\dfrac{3x}{11}+\dfrac{x}{10}$

● **18** $\dfrac{x}{2}+\dfrac{x}{3}+\dfrac{x}{4}$

● **19** $\dfrac{2x}{3}+\dfrac{2x}{5}+\dfrac{2x}{7}$

● **20** $\dfrac{x}{10}+\dfrac{x}{11}+\dfrac{x}{12}$

You can also have letters in the denominator as well as the numerator.
You can also have more than one term.

Examples

1 Simplify $\dfrac{2}{x}+\dfrac{7}{x}$

The denominators are the same so the fractions can be added straight away.

$$\dfrac{2}{x}+\dfrac{7}{x}=\dfrac{9}{x}$$

2 Simplify $\dfrac{x+3}{2}+\dfrac{x}{7}$

The common denominator is 14.

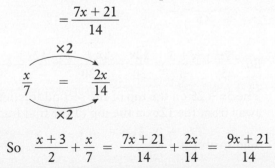

This bracket can be multiplied out. You saw this in Chapter 9.

$$=\dfrac{7x+21}{14}$$

So $\dfrac{x+3}{2}+\dfrac{x}{7}=\dfrac{7x+21}{14}+\dfrac{2x}{14}=\dfrac{9x+21}{14}$

Exercise 15:2

1 $\dfrac{2}{x} + \dfrac{5}{x}$

2 $\dfrac{3}{2x} + \dfrac{7}{2x}$

3 $\dfrac{4}{7x} + \dfrac{3}{7x}$

4 $\dfrac{3}{x+1} + \dfrac{4}{x+1}$

5 $\dfrac{6}{2x+3} + \dfrac{5}{2x+3}$

6 $\dfrac{x}{2} + \dfrac{x+1}{3}$

7 $\dfrac{x+1}{4} + \dfrac{x}{5}$

8 $\dfrac{x+4}{7} + \dfrac{x}{6}$

9 $\dfrac{x}{5} + \dfrac{2x+1}{4}$

10 $\dfrac{2x-3}{5} + \dfrac{x}{4}$

● 11 $\dfrac{x+2}{2} + \dfrac{x+3}{3}$

● 12 $\dfrac{2x+1}{2} + \dfrac{3x+1}{5}$

Subtracting fractions

Subtracting fractions is very similar to adding them.
If the fraction you are subtracting has more than one term you may need to put them in a bracket.

Example Simplify $\dfrac{2x}{5} - \dfrac{x+5}{6}$

The common denominator is 30.

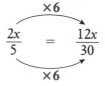

$$\dfrac{2x}{5} = \dfrac{12x}{30}$$

$$\dfrac{x+5}{6} = \dfrac{5(x+5)}{30} = \dfrac{5x+25}{30}$$

So $\dfrac{2x}{5} - \dfrac{x+5}{6} = \dfrac{12x}{30} - \dfrac{5x+25}{30} = \dfrac{12x - (5x+25)}{30}$

The $5x + 25$ on the top of the second fraction must *all* be taken away from the $12x$ on the top of the first fraction.

The answer is $\dfrac{7x - 25}{30}$

Exercise 15:3

1 $\dfrac{3x}{5} - \dfrac{x}{5}$ **5** $\dfrac{x}{4} - \dfrac{x}{8}$ **9** $\dfrac{x}{2} - \dfrac{x}{3}$ **● 13** $\dfrac{2x}{5} - \dfrac{x+1}{3}$

2 $\dfrac{2x}{7} - \dfrac{x}{7}$ **6** $\dfrac{x}{3} - \dfrac{x}{9}$ **10** $\dfrac{x}{3} - \dfrac{x}{5}$ **● 14** $\dfrac{3x}{7} - \dfrac{x+2}{4}$

3 $\dfrac{5x}{11} - \dfrac{2x}{11}$ **7** $\dfrac{2x}{5} - \dfrac{x}{10}$ **11** $\dfrac{2x}{3} - \dfrac{x}{4}$ **● 15** $\dfrac{5x}{6} - \dfrac{2x+1}{3}$

4 $\dfrac{x}{3} - \dfrac{x}{6}$ **8** $\dfrac{3x}{4} - \dfrac{3x}{8}$ **12** $\dfrac{3x}{5} - \dfrac{x}{7}$ **● 16** $\dfrac{3x+1}{2} - \dfrac{x+6}{5}$

Multiplying fractions

Multiplying algebraic fractions is easy.
You multiply the two numerators together and the two denominators together.
Simplify your answer if possible.

Example   **a** Simplify $\dfrac{x}{3} \times \dfrac{y}{8}$

$$\dfrac{x}{3} \times \dfrac{y}{8} = \dfrac{xy}{24}$$

           b Simplify $\dfrac{2x}{4} \times \dfrac{x}{7}$

$$\dfrac{2x}{4} \times \dfrac{x}{7} = \dfrac{2x^2}{28} \overset{\div 2}{\underset{\div 2}{=}} \dfrac{x^2}{14}$$

Exercise 15:4

1 $\dfrac{x}{2} \times \dfrac{y}{3}$ **5** $\dfrac{x}{2} \times \dfrac{x}{3}$ **9** $\dfrac{3}{x} \times \dfrac{2}{x}$

2 $\dfrac{x}{3} \times \dfrac{y}{4}$ **6** $\dfrac{x}{5} \times \dfrac{x}{4}$ **10** $\dfrac{4}{x} \times \dfrac{7}{x}$

3 $\dfrac{x}{5} \times \dfrac{y}{7}$ **7** $\dfrac{2x}{3} \times \dfrac{x}{7}$ **● 11** $\dfrac{4}{3x} \times \dfrac{3}{2x}$

4 $\dfrac{2x}{3} \times \dfrac{y}{5}$ **8** $\dfrac{2x}{7} \times \dfrac{3x}{5}$ **● 12** $\dfrac{4}{3x} \times \dfrac{7x}{2}$

Dividing fractions

The quick way to divide fractions is to turn the second fraction over then multiply.

Example Simplify $\dfrac{2x}{4} \div \dfrac{x+5}{7}$

$$\dfrac{2x}{4} \div \dfrac{x+5}{7} = \dfrac{2x}{4} \times \dfrac{7}{x+5} = \dfrac{14x}{4(x+5)} = \dfrac{14x}{4x+20} = \dfrac{7x}{2x+10}$$

Exercise 15:5

1 $\dfrac{x}{4} \div \dfrac{x}{3}$

2 $\dfrac{x}{3} \div \dfrac{x}{7}$

3 $\dfrac{x}{3} \div \dfrac{x}{5}$

4 $\dfrac{2x}{3} \div \dfrac{x}{5}$

5 $\dfrac{3x}{5} \div \dfrac{2x}{7}$

6 $\dfrac{5x}{7} \div \dfrac{x}{3}$

● **7** $\dfrac{x}{2} \div \dfrac{x+3}{5}$

● **8** $\dfrac{x}{3} \div \dfrac{x+2}{7}$

● **9** $\dfrac{x}{4} \div \dfrac{2x+1}{5}$

Sometimes, equations have fractions in them.
One way to solve them is to simplify the fractions first.

Example Solve $\dfrac{2x}{3} + \dfrac{x}{4} = 11$

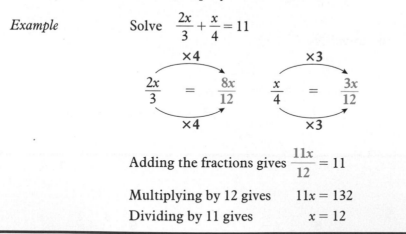

Adding the fractions gives $\dfrac{11x}{12} = 11$

Multiplying by 12 gives $11x = 132$

Dividing by 11 gives $x = 12$

Exercise 15:6

Solve these equations.

1 $\dfrac{x}{2} + \dfrac{x}{3} = 10$

2 $\dfrac{x}{3} + \dfrac{x}{4} = 56$

3 $\dfrac{x}{5} + \dfrac{x}{7} = 60$

4 $\dfrac{2x}{3} - \dfrac{x}{4} = 15$

5 $\dfrac{3x}{5} - \dfrac{x}{6} = 26$

6 $\dfrac{4x}{5} - \dfrac{x}{7} = 23$

● **7** $\dfrac{5x}{7} + \dfrac{2x}{6} = 22$

● **8** $\dfrac{3x}{5} + \dfrac{2x}{7} = 15.5$

2 Recurring decimals

One is not amused.

You have seen how to turn a fraction into a decimal.

If you have a fraction $\dfrac{a}{b}$ you divide a by b to turn the fraction into a decimal.

When you do this you will get
either   a decimal that stops
or   a recurring decimal.

Terminating decimal

A **terminating decimal** is one which stops.

    0.5, 0.867, 0.373 645 651 2 are all terminating decimals.

Recurring decimal

A **recurring decimal** is one which does not stop but which repeats.

$$\tfrac{1}{9} = 1 \div 9 = 0.111\,111\,111\ldots$$

The 1s carry on for ever.
$$0.111\,111\,111\ldots = 0.\dot{1}$$

$$\tfrac{1}{7} = 1 \div 7 = 0.142\,857\,142\,857\,142\,857\ldots$$

The 142 857 part carries on for ever.
$$0.142\,857\,142\,857\,142\,857\ldots = 0.\dot{1}4285\dot{7}$$

171

Exercise 15:7

 1 Work out the values of each of the fractions $\frac{1}{2}, \frac{1}{3}, \frac{1}{4}$, etc. up to $\frac{1}{20}$ as decimals.
Write each answer as a terminating or recurring decimal.

 2 **a** Write down the value of $\frac{1}{9}$ as a decimal.
 b Work out the decimal for each of these fractions.
   (1) $\frac{2}{9}$ (2) $\frac{3}{9}$ (3) $\frac{4}{9}$
 c Use your answers to **a** and **b** to write down the decimals for:
   (1) $\frac{5}{9}$ (2) $\frac{7}{9}$ (3) $\frac{8}{9}$
 d Explain how to write down the decimal for a fraction with a denominator of 9.

In the rest of this exercise use your calculator to work out the decimals.

3 **a** Work out the decimal for each of these fractions.
   (1) $\frac{1}{99}$ (3) $\frac{7}{99}$ (5) $\frac{29}{99}$
   (2) $\frac{2}{99}$ (4) $\frac{18}{99}$ (6) $\frac{70}{99}$
 b Use your answers to **a** to write down the decimals for:
   (1) $\frac{5}{99}$ (3) $\frac{35}{99}$ (5) $\frac{98}{99}$
   (2) $\frac{10}{99}$ (4) $\frac{76}{99}$ (6) $\frac{57}{99}$
 c Explain how to write down the decimal for a fraction with a denominator of 99.

4 **a** Work out the decimal for each of these fractions.
   (1) $\frac{1}{999}$ (3) $\frac{15}{999}$ (5) $\frac{123}{999}$
   (2) $\frac{2}{999}$ (4) $\frac{25}{999}$ (6) $\frac{350}{999}$
 b Use your answers to **a** to write down the decimals for:
   (1) $\frac{5}{999}$ (3) $\frac{58}{999}$ (5) $\frac{389}{999}$
   (2) $\frac{13}{999}$ (4) $\frac{250}{999}$ (6) $\frac{998}{999}$
 c Explain how to write down the decimal for a fraction with a denominator of 999.

You already know that every terminating decimal can be written as a fraction.
0.5 is 5 tenths because the 5 is in the tenths column.

So $0.5 = \frac{5}{10} = \frac{1}{2}$

$$\frac{5}{10} \xlongequal{\div 5} \frac{1}{2}$$
$\div 5$

0.32 is 32 hundredths because the 2 is in the hundredths column.

So $0.32 = \frac{32}{100} = \frac{8}{25}$

$$\frac{32}{100} \xlongequal{\div 4} \frac{8}{25}$$
$\div 4$

0.129 is 129 thousandths because the 9 is in the thousandths column.

So $0.129 = \frac{129}{1000}$

You may now realise that every recurring decimal can also be written as a fraction.

If the recurring part is a single digit
the fraction is that digit over 9

$0.\dot{2}$

$= \frac{2}{9}$

If the recurring part has two digits
the fraction is the two digits over 99

$0.\dot{3}\dot{1}$

$= \frac{31}{99}$

If the recurring part has three digits
the fraction is the three digits over 999

$0.\dot{4}8\dot{7}$

$= \frac{487}{999}$

and so on.

Exercise 15:8

1 Write these decimals as fractions. Write each fraction in its simplest form.

    a 0.3   **c** 0.375   **e** 0.4728   ● **g** 2.52

    b 0.56   **d** 0.275   **f** 0.1825   ● **h** 3.145

2   Write these recurring decimals as fractions.

   a $0.\dot{4}$ **c** $0.\ddot{4}\dot{1}$ **e** $0.2\dot{5}\dot{7}$ **g** $0.\dot{1}67\dot{3}$

   b $0.\dot{7}$ **d** $0.\dot{2}\dot{8}$ **f** $0.\dot{7}2\dot{7}$ **h** $0.\dot{1}344\dot{2}$

3   Write these recurring decimals as fractions.
Write each fraction in its simplest form.

   a $0.\dot{3}$ **c** $0.\dot{4}\dot{2}$ **e** $0.\dot{3}1\dot{2}$ **g** $0.8\dot{5}\dot{2}$

   b $0.\dot{6}$ **d** $0.\dot{2}\dot{7}$ **f** $0.\dot{2}3\dot{7}$ **h** $0.\dot{7}1\dot{7}$

4   Work out the decimal for each of these fractions.
Write down what you notice about the patterns of digits in your answers.

   a $\frac{1}{7}$ $\frac{2}{7}$ $\frac{3}{7}$ $\frac{4}{7}$ $\frac{5}{7}$ $\frac{6}{7}$

   b $\frac{1}{13}$ $\frac{2}{13}$ $\frac{3}{13}$ $\frac{4}{13}$ $\frac{5}{13}$ $\frac{6}{13}$ $\frac{7}{13}$ $\frac{8}{13}$ $\frac{9}{13}$ $\frac{10}{13}$ $\frac{11}{13}$ $\frac{12}{13}$

Here is an algebraic proof of why $0.\dot{4} = \frac{4}{9}$

You want to know what fraction is the same as $0.\dot{4}$ so start by saying $x = 0.\dot{4}$

So $x = 0.\dot{4}$
or $x = 0.444\,444\,444\,444 \ldots$

Now multiply both sides by 10
                      $10x = 4.444\,444\,444\,444 \ldots$

If you take these away, you get rid of the decimal part of the numbers.
$$10x = 4.444\,444\,444\,444 \ldots$$
$$-\,x = 0.444\,444\,444\,444 \ldots$$
$$9x = 4$$

So $x = \dfrac{4}{9}$

and you have proved that $0.\dot{4} = \frac{4}{9}$

---

5   Use the method above to prove that

   a $0.\dot{2} = \frac{2}{9}$ **b** $0.\dot{5} = \frac{5}{9}$ **c** $0.\dot{2}\dot{3} = \frac{23}{99}$

16 | Statistics: what does it all mean?

1 Averages

2 Scatter graphs

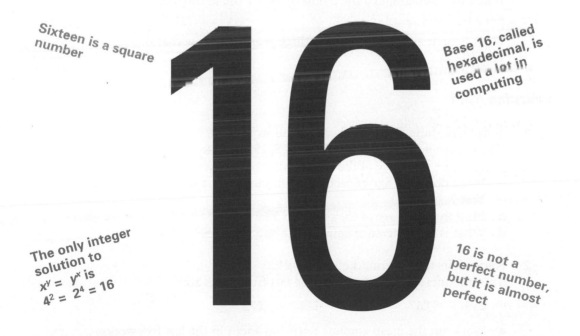

Sixteen is a square number

Base 16, called hexadecimal, is used a lot in computing

The only integer solution to
$x^y = y^x$ is
$4^2 = 2^4 = 16$

16 is not a perfect number, but it is almost perfect

1 Averages

These two photographs were taken three years apart.

When we photographed the pupils in Year 7 the average age
was 11.4 years.

What is their average age exactly three years later now that they are in
Year 10?

Exercise 16:1

1 Tony, Tim, Julie, Paul and Aisha are all in Year 10.
Their ages on January 1st are 14, 14, 15, 15, and 14.
   a Find the mean age of the five pupils.
   b Write down the age of each pupil on January 1st when they were in
Year 7.
   c Find the mean age of the pupils in Year 7.
   d What is the difference between the two averages?

2 Katie visits the supermarket each week.
The amounts she has spent over the last five weeks are:

   £53   £67   £64   £81   £72

   a Work out the mean amount Katie has spent in the last five weeks.
   b The supermarket gives out £5 off vouchers for regular customers.
   Work out how much Katie would have spent each week if she had
   used one voucher each week.
   c Work out the mean amount Katie would have spent if she had used
   a voucher each week.
   d What is the difference between the two means?

If a fixed amount is added to every value in a set of data, then the mean will increase by the same amount.

Example The mean of the numbers   14   15   17   19   24   31   is

$$\frac{14 + 15 + 17 + 19 + 24 + 31}{6} = 20$$

If 7 is added to each data value the values become

21   22   24   26   31   38

The mean of these new values is

$$\frac{21 + 22 + 24 + 26 + 31 + 38}{6} = 27$$

As you can see, the mean has increased by 7.

3   The mean age of the pupils in class 7R is 11.7 years.
     What will the average age be when they become 10R?

4   The mean time taken to run a 100 m race by the girls in 7R is
     15.8 seconds.
     By the time they are in Year 8 they have all knocked 1 second off their
     time.
     What is their new mean time?

5   The number of chocolates in 50 boxes of mint sticks is shown in
     the table.

Number of chocolates in a box	Number of boxes
48	6
49	8
50	28
51	5
52	3

   a Work out the mean number of chocolates in a box. Give your answer
      to 2 dp.
   b During a '10% extra free' offer, five extra chocolates are added to
      each box.
      What is the mean of these 50 boxes with the extra chocolates in
      them?

Exercise 16:2

1 Write down what you think happens to the mode when all the values in a set of data are increased or decreased by a fixed amount.

2 Use these sets of data to test your theory.
(1) 5 8 7 9 16 8 7 9 5 8 1 13 14 15 8 5 4
(2) 23.1 25.8 23.1 24.6 24.6 23.1 24.9 25.8 21.9 23.5
 a Find the mode of each of these sets of data.
 b Add 6 to each data value.
 c Find the mode of the new values.

3 Write down what you think happens to the median when all the values in a set of data are increased or decreased by a fixed amount.

4 Use the sets of data in question **2** to test your theory.

5 Copy these sentences. Fill in the gaps.

If a fixed amount is added to or subtracted from every value in a set of data, then the mode will ....

If a fixed amount is added to or subtracted from every value in a set of data, then the median will ....

Multiplication and Division

Exercise 16:3

1 a Find the mean of the numbers   18   26   24   19   23   24   28   24
 b Multiply all the numbers by 3 and write down their new values.
 c Find the mean of the new set of numbers.
 d Describe what has happened to the mean when every data value has been multiplied by 3.

2 a Divide all the numbers in question **1** by 2 and write down their new values.
 b Find the mean of the new set of numbers.
 c Describe what has happened to the mean when every data value has been divided by 2.

3 Write down what you think happens to the mode when all the values in a set of data are multiplied or divided by a fixed number.

4 Use these sets of data to test your theory from question **3**.
 a 5 8 7 9 16 8 7 9 5 8 1 13 14 15 8 5 4
 b 23.1 25.8 23.1 24.6 24.6 23.1 24.9 25.8 21.9 23.5

5 Write down what you think happens to the median when all the values in a set of data are multiplied or divided by a fixed number.

6 Use the sets of data in question **4** to test your theory from question **5**.

7 Copy these sentences. Fill in the gaps.

If every value in a set of data is multiplied or divided by a fixed number, then the mode will ....

If every value in a set of data is multiplied or divided by a fixed number, then the median will ....

8 A bottling machine in a drinks factory is set to fill bottles with exactly 220 ml of orange juice.
 The trading standards inspector takes a random sample of 100 bottles. His results are shown in the table.

Amount of juice in bottle (ml)	Number of bottles
218	7
219	15
220	68
221	9
222	1

 a Find the mean amount in each bottle. Give your answer to 1 dp.
 b The amount in each bottle is increased by 10%.
    Draw a new table, increasing the amount in each bottle by 10%.
 c Work out the mean from your new data.
 d Has the mean increased by 10%?

The range

Range	For any set of data, the **range** is the biggest value take away the smallest value.

The range measures the spread of a set of data. The bigger the range, the more spread out the data is.

Exercise 16:4

1 Find the range of this set of data.

15 18 23 9 26 15 12
45 25 36 12 18 15 17

2 Five is added to each of the data values.
What is the new range?

3 Nine is subtracted from each of the
data values.
What is the new range?

4 Each of the data values is multiplied by 4.
What is the new range?

5 Each of the data values is divided by 5.
What is the new range?

6 Copy and complete this table.

Operation	Effect on the range
adding a fixed amount n subtracting a fixed amount n multiplying by a fixed amount n dividing by a fixed amount n	

7 **a** Use the data values n $n+1$ $n+2$ $n+3$ $n+4$ $n+5$
to show that the range is increased by a factor of 3 when each of the data values is multiplied by 3.
b Use the same data values to show that the range is increased by a factor m when each of the data values is multiplied by m.

2 Scatter graphs

Anne is the Head of the Maths department at Adhamup School.

She is looking at the test results of some of her pupils.

She is comparing them with their results in other subjects.

She decides to draw some scatter graphs to help her compare the results.

Anne starts by comparing the Maths results with the Science results.
She thinks these should be similar.

Scatter graph

A **scatter graph** is a diagram that is used to see if there is a connection between two sets of data.
One value goes on the *x* axis and the other on the *y* axis. It does not matter which way round they go.

This is a scatter graph showing test results in Maths and Science. One pupil scored 35 in Maths and 40 in Science. A point is plotted at (**35, 40**).

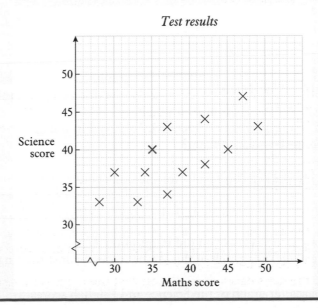

Test results

Exercise 16:5

1 Here are some of the results for class 7P in Maths and Science.

Maths	27	34	26	28	34	27	40	21	35	27	29
Science	29	38	22	29	27	32	43	20	32	25	31

a Copy these axes on to graph paper.

b The first column in the table shows that a pupil scored **27** in Maths and **29** in Science.
Plot a point at **(27, 29)** on your graph.

c The second pupil scored **34** in Maths and **38** in Science.
Plot a point at (34, 38).

d Plot the rest of the points on your graph.

e Notice how the points are roughly in a line going from the bottom left to the top right of your graph.
Do you think that a student who did well in the Maths exam also did well in the Science exam?

2 These are the English results for the same students in 7P.

English	35	40	20	22	28	21	35	29	30	26	40

a Draw some axes as you did in question **1**.
b Draw a scatter graph of the Maths scores against the English scores.

● 3 Draw a scatter graph of the Science and English scores.

| Correlation | **Correlation** is a measurement of how strongly connected the two sets of data are. There are different types of correlation. |

| Positive correlation | This scatter graph shows the weights and heights of people. As the weight increases so does the height. This is **positive correlation**. |

Height

Weight

| Negative correlation | This graph shows the values of cars and their ages. As age increases, value decreases. This is **negative correlation**. |

Value of car

Age of car

| Zero correlation | This graph shows the height of some students against their maths scores. There is no connection between these two things. This is **zero correlation**. |

Height

Maths score

Correlation can also be strong or weak:

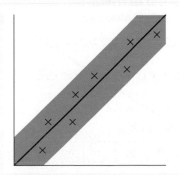

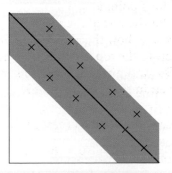

Strong correlation
The points all lie close to the line.

Weak correlation
The points are well spread out but still show a trend.

Exercise 16:6

1 The ages of ten Ford Escorts and their sale values are shown in this table.

Age (years)	3	6	5	4	2	6	5	3	6	5
Value (£)	6000	2500	2900	3500	6500	2300	3100	5800	2100	3300

a Plot a scatter graph to show this data.
b Describe the type of correlation that this data shows.
Choose from strong/weak and positive/negative.

2 Two judges awarded marks in an art competition.
Judge A scored out of 20. Judge B scored out of 15.
Here are the results of the judging for 10 paintings.

Judge A	15	12	8	19	7	6	17	8	15	16
Judge B	12	9	7	13	8	3	12	5	12	14

a Plot a scatter graph to show this data.
b Describe the type of correlation that this data shows.

Estimating values

If two sets of data show correlation, you can use your scatter graph to estimate missing values. You can draw a line that goes through the middle of the points.
The line is called a **line of best fit**.
This line can be used to estimate other data values.
To do this draw from one axis to the line of best fit and then to the other axis.

Example
Ben scored **32** in Maths but missed the Science test.
Work out an estimate for his Science score.
(1) Find 32 on the Maths axis.
(2) Draw a line up to the line of best fit.
(3) Draw across to the Science axis.
(4) Read off the Science score.
The estimate is shown by the **red** line on the graph.
The estimate for Ben's Science score is **34**.

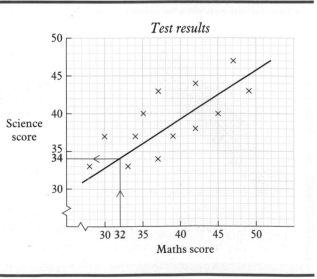

---

3   Look back at the scatter graph you drew in question **1**.
   a   Draw a line of best fit on your graph.
   b   Estimate the age of a car that is worth £5500.
   c   Estimate the value of a $3\frac{1}{2}$ year-old car.

4   Look back at the scatter graph you drew in question **2**.
   a   Draw a line of best fit on your graph.
   b   Judge A gives a piece of work 14 marks. Estimate the score Judge B would give.

5   LoPrice supermarkets are doing a survey of their customers.

   They asked how many visits people made to the supermarket during a three month period. They also asked how far away from the store the people lived.

   Here are the results for 14 customers.

Number of visits	9	7	12	11	14	12	6
Length of journey (miles)	7	5	5	8	3	4	8

Number of visits	8	15	13	5	12	2	9
Length of journey (miles)	5	3	6	10	1	7	6

   a   Plot a scatter graph to show this data.
   b   Draw on a line of best fit.
   c   Describe the type of correlation that this data shows.
   d   Estimate the number of visits made by a shopper living 9 miles away.
   e   Say how reliable you think this estimate is.
         What other factors could affect your answer?

Exercise 16:7

This scatter graph shows the number of CDs sold in the UK in the first half of the 1990s and the number of deaths in road accidents in Derbyshire during the same period.

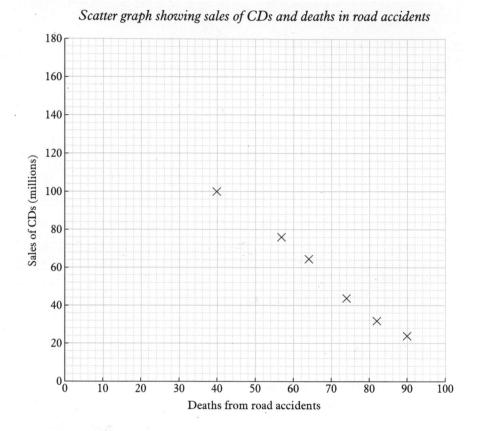

Scatter graph showing sales of CDs and deaths in road accidents

1   What type of correlation does this scatter graph show?

2   Copy the scatter graph and add a line of best fit.

3   How many CDs would have to be sold for deaths from road accidents to be eliminated completely?

4   Why do you think these two variables appear to be correlated?

5   It is clear that these two variables have no effect on each other.
   a Write down a variable that would be truly correlated with the sales of CDs.
   b Write down a variable that would be correlated with the number of deaths from road accidents.